In the Wake of the Crisis

In the Wake of the Crisis

Leading Economists Reassess Economic Policy

edited by Olivier Blanchard, David Romer,
Michael Spence, and Joseph Stiglitz

The MIT Press
Cambridge, Massachusetts
London, England

MIT Press books may be purchased at special quantity discounts for business or sales promotional use. For information, please email special_sales@mitpress.mit.edu or write to Special Sales Department, The MIT Press, 55 Hayward Street, Cambridge, MA 02142.

This book was set in Sabon by Toppan Best-set Premedia Limited. Printed and bound in the United States of America.

Library of Congress Cataloging-in-Publication Data

In the wake of the crisis : leading economists reassess economic policy / edited by Olivier Blanchard . . . [et al.].
    p.   cm.
Conference proceedings.
Includes bibliographical references and index.
ISBN 978-0-262-01761-9 (hardcover : alk. paper)
1. Global Financial Crisis, 2008–2009—Congresses. 2. Fiscal policy—Congresses. 3. Monetary policy—Congresses. 4. Economic development—Congresses. I. Blanchard, Olivier.
HB37172008.I6   2012
339.5—dc23

                                                                        2011040553

10 9 8 7 6 5 4 3 2 1

Contents

Preface

As a world economic crisis developed in 2008 and lasted longer than most economists predicted, it became increasingly clear that beliefs about macroeconomics and macroeconomic policy needed to be thoroughly examined. In the throes of the crisis, policymakers had to improvise. What should be done when interest rates reach the zero floor? How is liquidity best provided to segmented financial institutions and markets? How much should fiscal policy be used when starting from high levels of debt?

After the initial fires were put out, many questions remained. Is inflation targeting the right way to conduct policy, or should the monetary authority watch a larger set of targets? Should central bankers develop and use new tools, so-called macroprudential instruments? Could fiscal policy be used more efficiently? Were the precrisis targets for public debt the right ones? Should there be limits on current-account imbalances? Should countries use capital controls? Should there be better mechanisms to deliver global liquidity? What, if anything, can policymakers do to turn anemic recoveries into robust ones?

We at the International Monetary Fund badly needed answers or at least beginnings of answers to these questions. To begin the process, David Romer, Michael Spence, and Joseph Stiglitz helped me organize a conference at the IMF on March 7–8, 2011, for prominent academics and policymakers. We organized the Conference on Macro and Growth Policies in the Wake of the Crisis around six themes—monetary policy, fiscal policy, financial regulation, capital-account management, growth strategies, and the international monetary system. For each theme, David and I wrote a short note that listed some questions on the topic. We asked for views on these themes, not for formal papers. The conference proceedings are published in this book. They include the notes we wrote for each session, the contributions from the panelists, and my concluding remarks.

By the end of this fascinating conference, we knew that we had entered a brave new world and that the crisis is generating enough questions to fill our research agendas for years to come. It will take many years to uncover the answers. I am hopeful that this book contributes to the journey.

Organizing a major conference, getting very busy authors to write their contributions in time, correcting their mistakes in style and thinking, and getting the book out less than a year after the conference took place is a remarkable achievement. We are deeply thankful to Tracey Lookadoo and her team at the IMF for organizing the conference, to the MIT Press for going all-out to deliver on time, and especially to Josh Felman for his contribution from beginning to end.

Olivier Blanchard

I

Monetary Policy

Questions: How Should the Crisis Affect Our Views of Monetary Policy?

Precrisis Consensus

The years before the world economic crisis began in 2007 and 2008 saw the emergence of a consensus view of monetary policy. It went roughly like this:

1. Flexible inflation targeting provides a sound framework for monetary policy.

2. The supervisory and macroeconomic aspects of monetary policy can be largely separated.

3. Departures of asset prices from fundamentals are hard to detect in real time, and the contractionary effects of sharp falls in asset prices can be greatly mitigated by monetary easing. As a result, asset prices should affect monetary policy only to the extent that they help predict goods price inflation and the output gap.

4. The zero lower bound on nominal interest rates is a minor issue. It is rarely encountered, and its consequences are likely to be modest when it is. Moreover, policymakers have powerful tools (such as targeting long-term rates and temporarily raising their inflation target) that they can use if it becomes a major constraint.

5. Monetary policy and fiscal policy are linked in the long run through the government budget constraint, but in the medium run they should and can be kept largely separate.

Postcrisis Issues Related to the Precrisis Consensus

The crisis and the policy responses to it have raised concerns about each of these ingredients of the consensus view. Taking them in reverse order:

5. To what extent have policy actions in the crisis—such as special lending facilities, measures to prevent the disorderly failure of particular financial institutions, and actions to support sovereign debt—blurred the lines between monetary and fiscal policy? Are such actions a mistake? Are they necessary in extreme circumstances? Should they be a standard part of the monetary policy toolkit?

4. Has the zero lower bound been an important constraint in the crisis? Does the failure of central banks to adopt some of the precrisis ideas for dealing with the zero lower bound reflect drawbacks of those ideas that were not understood by their proponents, or does it reflect excessive caution or lack of concern about unemployment on the part of policy-makers? Should any of those ideas be adopted now? Should central banks adopt higher inflation targets when the crisis has passed? Should they target a price-level path or a path of nominal gross domestic product?

3. Should interest-rate policy respond to asset prices? If so, what asset prices—and what types of movements in those prices—should affect policy? Should central banks take a more ecumenical view of monetary policy, thinking not only of the policy rate but also of margin, reserve, downpayment, and capital requirements jointly as the tools of macro-economic and financial stabilization policy (as many of them once were)?

2. Is it important for central banks to play a major role in financial supervision? Should changes in capital requirements and related tools be coordinated with interest-rate policy? Can regulation of systematic risk and supervision of idiosyncratic risk be separated? If central banks use a larger set of tools beyond the policy rate, can full central-bank independence be preserved, or does it need to be redefined?

1. Is inflation targeting the right framework going forward? Is the so-called divine coincidence result that stable inflation implies a stable output gap a reasonable approximation, or should central banks explicitly care about the output gap? And if so, how? Also, even when they claim to follow an inflation-targeting strategy, central banks in many emerging economies clearly care about exchange-rate movements beyond their effect on inflation. Many of them use the policy rate and manage their reserves to smooth their exchange rate. Are they right to do so?

Other Issues Raised by the Crisis

Some other issues concerning monetary policy raised by the crisis:

1. Do large expansions of central-bank balance sheets pose a significant risk of inflation? If so, through what channel: A largely conventional one of losing sight of the inflation objective and of long and variable lags? A loss of confidence in central banks and a consequent unmooring of inflation expectations? Capital losses on central banks' balance sheets and a resulting loss of independence?

2. Is there any truth to the claim that central banks responded much more aggressively and creatively to disruptions in financial markets than to the prospect of years of high unemployment? If so, was this appropriate? And if it did occur and was not appropriate, why did it occur?

3. Do the increasingly precarious fiscal positions of many countries threaten central-bank independence?

4. How has the crisis changed the importance of international coordination in monetary policy? For example, swap lines and other arrangements among central banks were important during the crisis. And at the zero lower bound, a central bank cannot easily offset the aggregate demand effects of other countries' exchange rates or trade policies. Do these observations have important implications going forward?

5. Should central banks change their communication policies substantially as a result of the crisis?

1

Monetary Policy in the Wake of the Crisis

Olivier Blanchard

Before the economic crisis began in 2008, mainstream economists and policymakers had converged on a beautiful construction for monetary policy. To caricature just a bit: we had convinced ourselves that there was one target, inflation, and one instrument, the policy rate. And that was basically enough to get things done.

One lesson to be drawn from this crisis is that this construction was not right: beauty is not always synonymous with truth. There are many targets and many instruments. How the instruments are mapped onto the targets and how these instruments are best used are complicated problems, but we need to solve them. Future monetary policy is likely to be much messier than the simple construction we developed earlier.

Figure 1.1 shows the way that monetary policy was seen in advanced countries before the crisis. There was one target, stable inflation, and there was one instrument, the policy rate or more precisely the policy-rate rule, and that was basically enough. If you had the right rule for the policy rate, you would achieve low and stable inflation. The use of a rule, implicit or explicit, gave the central bank credibility and delivered a stable economy.

The implicit assumption was that stable inflation would deliver economic stability in the sense of a stable output gap. This was the case in many formal academic models, particularly in the benchmark new Keynesian model, which displayed a property that Jordi Gali and I have called the "divine coincidence." In these models, if you maintained stable inflation, you would also maintain a stable output gap. The two went together, so there was no reason to look at the output gap separately.

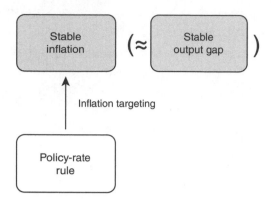

Figure 1.1
Precrisis orthodoxy: Inflation targeting.

Realism on the part of central bankers made them realize that this was an extreme proposition, that there could be (at least in the short run) some distance between the two, and that they also had to worry about the output gap. That led to something called *flexible inflation targeting*, in which central banks allowed for temporary deviations from the inflation target to stabilize what they thought was the output gap.

We learned two main lessons from the current crisis. The first is that even with stable inflation and a stable output gap, things might not be going well behind the—macroeconomic—scene. For example, tensions can build up in the financial sector, and financial instability eventually translates into major problems in terms of output and activity. This realization has led to a general consensus that the list of targets must now include financial stability as well as macroeconomic stability.

There is also agreement that the debate as it was framed precrisis— whether you should use the policy rate to try to achieve both macro- and financial stability—was not the right debate. There are many instruments out there, not just the policy rate, and there is no reason to rely only on the policy rate.

The second lesson is that the link between inflation stability and the output gap is probably much weaker than was originally thought. In a number of countries, the behavior of inflation appears to have become increasingly divorced from the evolution of the output gap. (This is hard to prove, given that potential output and, by implication, the output gap are unobservable.) If this is the case, then central bankers who care about macrostability cannot be content just to keep inflation stable. They have to watch both inflation and the output gap, measured as best as they can. Nobody will watch the output gap for them.

At a conference attended by many central bankers recently, I got the sense that the emerging consensus among central bankers (though not necessarily among academics) was that there were now two tasks—(1) to maintain macrostability by pursuing monetary policy in the same way as before, using a rule for the policy rate, and perhaps giving more weight to the output gap, and (2) to maintain financial stability using macroprudential tools. I also got the sense that they thought these two activities could be kept largely separate. Maybe one institution could do one, and another institution could do the other. There had to be some interaction between the two, but they could be largely separate. This way of thinking about policy is captured in figure 1.2.

But this view might be too neat a view—two targets, each with its own instrument. First, the mapping of macroprudential policies onto the target of financial stability is complex. Macroprudential policy has to be about many aspects of the financial system, and the notion that we can find one sufficient statistic for systemic risk that we can then target is probably an illusion. We are going to have to look all the time at the balance sheets of the various financial institutions to identify the risks that are building up. In figure 1.3, many arrows (not just one) start from

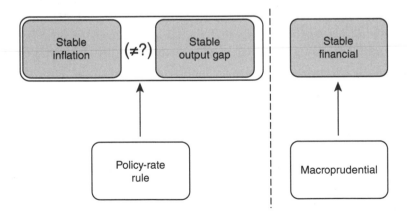

Figure 1.2
Postcrisis: This way?

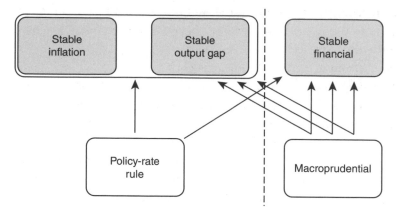

Figure 1.3
Or that way?

the macroprudential box. Second, there are strong interactions between macroprudential instruments and the policy rate. The empirical evidence suggests that low policy rates lead to excessive risk taking, thus requiring the use of macroprudential tools. And macroprudential tools have macroeconomic effects: a higher loan-to-value ratio affects housing investment and thus gross domestic product. This leads me to think of policy as in figure 1.3, with many arrows going up and also sideways—from the policy rate to financial stability and from macroprudential tools to macrostability.

Figure 1.3 is much less neat than figure 1.2, but I believe it is a better description of how policy will have to operate. We need to think about monetary policy in a broad sense as having many targets—at least inflation, output, and risk—and having many instruments. We can have some allocation of instruments, but we must also realize that most instruments are going to affect all three targets in some way. This raises many issues, including the following:

• How these macroprudential tools can be used is something we know relatively little about. We talk about varying the maximum loan-to-value ratio to stabilize house prices, but how such a ratio actually affects housing prices and housing investment, in a reliable way, remains to be worked out. The same holds for most of the other macroprudential instruments. So a large amount of work remains to be done.

- Political economy issues loom large. When the main tool of monetary policy was the policy rate, monetary policy was perceived as fairly neutral with respect to sectors and particular groups. (Even the policy rate is far from neutral in that way, but somehow nobody complains.) So the danger that an independent central bank could target, to help or to hurt, a specific sector or group was seen as low. But if central banks start being in charge of many instruments, nearly all of them having an effect on a specific segment of the economy, then the question of independence comes up. The interactions between the various instruments and objectives argue for one decider, presumably the central bank. But how much independence you then can give to it is an open question.
- Finally, the notion that the central bank uses many instruments reminds one of earlier monetary policies, such as those of the 1950s, in which too many tools and too many interventions led to distortions and sometimes perverse outcomes. This is a challenge. Still, we have to accept the fact that monetary policy should probably be thought of in that form—many instruments and many targets.

Let me end with remarks about monetary policy in emerging-market countries, focusing on the role of the exchange rate in monetary policy. Before the crisis, many emerging-market countries had adopted inflation targeting. This was seen as state-of-the-art monetary policy, and there was strong pressure to adopt it.

These countries described themselves as floaters. They argued that they cared about the exchange rate only to the extent that it affected inflation, and so as part of inflation targeting they took into account the effect of the exchange rate on inflation. But they put no weight on the exchange rate as a target. This way of describing policy is captured in figure 1.4. These were their words, but their deeds, in many cases, were often quite different. Most inflation targeters cared deeply about the exchange rate, beyond just its effect on inflation, and this affected monetary policy.

It is my sense that the deeds were right, not the words. But the discrepancy between words and deeds resulted in a confusing message.

Countries have reasons to care about their exchange rate. There is such a thing as too low or too high an exchange rate, and to the

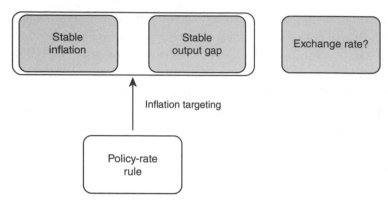

Figure 1.4
Precrisis: Inflation targeting in emerging-market countries

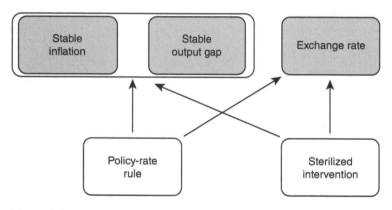

Figure 1.5
Postcrisis: A more explicit approach?

usual targets of stable inflation and stable output gap should be added an exchange-rate target, either the level of the exchange rate or its rate of change. (Why and which one it should be are important but get into issues I do not take up here.)

Following the same logic used earlier, we should not think of one tool as being able to do everything, which it cannot. We should think of two tools—the policy rate and sterilized intervention, which works when there is imperfect capital mobility. This way of thinking about policy is represented in figure 1.5. How these two tools can be used, how they should be used, how this depends on the degree of financial openness, and how central banks should communicate the logic of their policies (rather than continue to pretend that they do not care about the exchange rate) is yet another challenge, both for researchers and for central bankers.

Let me conclude by repeating my basic message. We have moved from a one-target, one-instrument world to one where there are many targets and many instruments. And we are just starting to begin the long and difficult process of exploring what such a new framework may look like.

2

Conventional Wisdom Challenged? Monetary Policy after the Crisis

Guillermo Ortiz

As Olivier Blanchard has pointed out, the global economic crisis of the early twenty-first century has challenged some aspects of the conventional wisdom regarding the conceptual framework and implementation of monetary policy. In my view, it has also reinforced the case for continuing the implementation of other aspects. Although the epicenter of the crisis was in the developed world, I believe that relevant lessons can be taken from previous emerging-market crises. In this chapter, I examine some of these lessons and discuss my own views.

Inflation Targeting

During the global economic crisis of 2008, emerging markets showed more resilience than advanced economies, and by 2011 they were exiting the global crisis at a much faster pace than advanced economies (figure 2.1). This reflects sizable government policy support, favorable external conditions, and solid macroeconomic policy fundamentals that proved helpful before, during, and after the global financial turmoil.

Since the crises of the 1990s and early 2000s, most emerging markets have imposed much stronger policy frameworks (figure 2.2). This was of course facilitated by a benign external environment characterized by positive terms of trade effects. To achieve economic stability and sustained growth, they

- Strengthened fiscal positions and increased international reserves,
- Developed domestic capital markets, and
- Developed a consistent framework of monetary and exchange-rate policies with flexible exchange rates and inflation targeting.

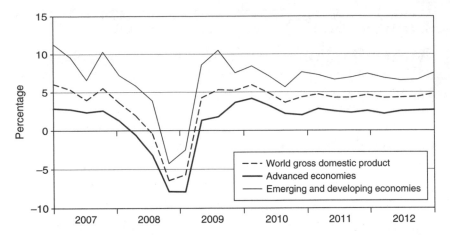

Figure 2.1
Global gross domestic product growth (percentage, quarter over quarter, annualized). *Source:* International Monetary Fund, *World Economic Outlook Update,* January 2011.

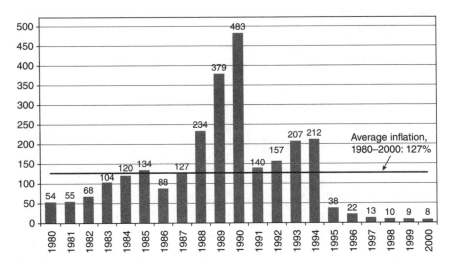

Figure 2.2
Inflation in Latin America and the Caribbean (percentage change, average consumer prices). *Source:* International Monetary Fund, World Economic Outlook database, October 2010.

Academic research has documented that the "great moderation," the reduction of fiscal dominance (greatly helped by the reduction of the debt overhang of the 1980s after the Brady Plan) and the adoption of inflation targeting, was very helpful in reducing inflation in emerging markets, particularly in Latin America, which was an inflation-prone region.[1] The average inflation rate in Latin America was 136 percent per year in the 1980s and 240 percent per year in the first half of the 1990s. Brazil's inflation rate exceeded 1,000 percent per year in five of the six years between 1989 and 1994. Inflation in the region did not begin to moderate until the mid-1990s: it averaged less than 20 percent per year from 1995 to 1999 and only 7 percent from 2000 to 2009.[2]

Some inflation-targeting central banks may have paid little attention to monetary aggregates, credit expansion, and leverage of households and businesses. Its operational simplicity may have provided the wrong view to some policymakers, in the sense that implementing monetary policy was almost mechanical. The models that were developed to guide central banks' decisions under inflation targeting did not explicitly develop a nontrivial financial sector, so the issue of financial shocks to the real economy was not explicitly considered. Thus, economists need to build up better analytical tools for understanding interactions between the real sector and the financial system, among markets and institutions, and between monetary policy and macroprudential tools.

One positive lesson that emerged from the recent crisis was the effectiveness of the inflation-targeting framework, particularly in emerging markets. Although the crisis prompted large relative price adjustments, inflation remained under control. Recent research shows that, relative to other countries, inflation-targeting countries were able to maintain better anchored inflation expectations during the crisis and, with their flexible exchange-rate regimes, saw sharp real depreciations that helped reduce the output contraction.[3]

Early in the crisis, the Mexican peso depreciated sharply against the U.S. dollar, and more recently, commodity prices have increased dramatically. However, inflation in Mexico has remained under control while expectations remain anchored. The inflation-targeting framework and the credibility gained over the years through a solid fiscal stance and a well-capitalized financial system have ensured that Mexico's central bank can adjust its policy stance in response to business-cycle fluctuations. Of course, access to the newly created Flexible Credit Line (FCL) and the swap lines from the U.S. Federal Reserve helped to strengthen the reserve position during the crisis (thus reducing perceived country risk). This was a radical departure from previous episodes, which resulted in inflation and severe financial dislocations.

Most emerging-market inflation targeters have intervened recurrently in the foreign-exchange market before, during, and after the crisis. The objectives have varied depending on each country's circumstances. Interventions have generally aimed to reduce exchange-rate volatility, smooth abrupt exchange-rate fluctuations, and accumulate (or in some cases reduce) international reserves. This issue has generated considerable discussion (and confusion) and given rise to the notion of "fear of floating," since exchange-rate intervention is at odds with the theoretical framework of inflation targeting. Most emerging-market exchange-rate interventions have not aimed at targeting a certain level of the exchange rate because it is not possible to achieve two targets with one instrument. However, the most recent episode of the so-called currency wars has revived this issue. In my opinion, the more frequent and intense interventions recently observed in the foreign-exchange market reflect the different macroconditions and speeds of recovery in developed and emerging markets. They also reflect the increasing importance of China's exchange-rate policy in influencing monetary and exchange-rate policy in other emerging markets, particularly in Asia.

Emerging countries did not experience the constraint of the zero lower bound for interest rates because the risk of deflation was never the threat that it is in developed countries. Central banks in developed countries have been able to offer a toolkit (such as quantitative easing and price-level targeting) to fight the zero-bound constraint, but the risks of the zero-bound constraint should not be minimized. Because the risks of ensuring price stability are asymmetric, central bankers are better equipped to fight inflation than deflation.

These instruments are not necessarily useful for overcoming the zero-bound constraint, so we are fortunate that the toolkit was not fully tested. But no central bank (not even Japan's) opted for changing the inflation target or targeting a price level. These instruments could overcome the zero-bound constraint by making the real rate negative, but the long-term consequences of these policy decisions are less clear. In fact, the strategy to undo quantitative easing remains untested, and inflation risks persist in the eyes of many observers.

Financial Stability and the Role of Central Banks in Banking Supervision

For emerging markets, the great crisis of 2008 and 2009 was a fundamental stress test—of the ability of the domestic financial system to withstand a global financial crisis and of the ability of the real economy to absorb a very large shock and to experience a sharp policy-induced rebound. No emerging-market economy in Asia or Latin America that suffered a financial crisis in the 1990s and early part of this century suffered a domestic financial crisis as a consequence of the global crisis. This remarkable situation shows that emerging markets learned from their mistakes. Their banks did not load up with toxic assets and were well capitalized heading into the crisis.

Given the nature of emerging-market crises, policymakers focused on macroprudential considerations in the aftermath of these episodes. They may not have done so by establishing a formal macroprudential framework (as is being done today in several countries), but they implemented preventive regulations, such as avoiding the currency mismatches and excessive leverage that led to credit booms and collapses in previous episodes. That is a missing piece in Olivier Blanchard's graphs of the monetary framework in emerging markets (see chapter 1).

The great crisis was a massive institutional failure, involving financial institutions, regulators, rating agencies, and international organizations. A deficient regulatory and supervisory framework for the financial system at an international level reflected the widespread belief that market discipline (and its pillars) was sufficient to promote financial stability, even in the absence of a strong framework for financial regulation and supervision.

The crisis showed that price stability alone does not imply financial stability. Lightly regulated financial markets that are subject to the forces of market discipline are not sufficient for allocating resources effectively and managing risk. In addition, the global financial crisis demonstrated that the financial system tends to reinforce the economic cycles, a bias that is amplified today by the highly interconnected nature of financial institutions and markets.

Therefore, the role of central banks as guardians of financial stability must be rethought, much as has happened in many emerging markets after their financial crises. This has been the subject of much discussion and debate in academic and multilateral forums, with particular attention paid to central banks' involvement in the design of financial regulation and in banking supervision. Central banks need to have a bank supervisory responsibility that reinforces their responsibilities for ensuring the stability of financial systems (like the central bank of Canada).

Nevertheless, the central bank's supervisory role should not interfere with its independence in conducting monetary policy. Although central banks justifiably oversee the payment systems and market positions, which have a direct effect on the stability of the financial system, allowing them to take a much broader responsibility (such as supervising banks or the capital adequacy of banks) can distort the conduct of monetary policy and eventually blur the role of monetary and fiscal policies.

A government institution should undertake the broader role of bank resolution. Since these institutions usually determine when to intervene or recapitalize banks, they should be part of the government. These institutions should have the means to carry out their mandate. Only fiscal policy can be burdened with these permanent interventions.

Asset-Price Targeting

Another lesson from the crisis is the need to consider asset-price targeting. The housing bubble in the United States, the United Kingdom, Ireland, and Spain is one example. Two questions seem key to this ongoing debate:

- First, were monetary authorities too complacent, easing too much for too long?
- Second, can central bankers identify and disinflate asset bubbles while avoiding the business-cycle side effects?

If excessive looseness was the root of the financial crisis, then authorities failed to normalize on time, and there probably is no need to introduce explicit asset-price targets for central banks. But if monetary policy was not the cause and the asset-price bubbles were exogenous, then there could be an argument for targeting asset prices. The answer probably lies somewhere between these two perspectives and varies from case to case.

Even if central banks are mandated to target asset prices, the operational aspects could complicate monetary policy immensely and may well result in conflicts between objectives. The difficulty is twofold—to identify asset-price bubbles and to stabilize asset prices while minimizing their negative effects on the business cycle. Although desirable, it is not clear that asset prices should be targeted explicitly. A challenge for central banks and regulators is to develop early warning indicators that bubbles are forming in asset prices so that authorities can try to mitigate them.

One alternative is to deal with asset-price bubbles in the framework of macroprudential policies in which central banks must play a central role. The appropriate tools for dealing with bubbles may require an array of measures (including margins, reserves, and credit limits), many of which are being currently applied by several Asian countries that are experiencing property bubbles. One important lesson on this subject is pragmatism—the willingness to prevent and overcome political or special interests that often are behind the formation of bubbles.

Monetary and Fiscal Policies

The special lending facilities to the financial sector and to sovereign debt support (such as the ones undertaken by the U.S. Federal Reserve and the European Central Bank) have blurred the boundaries between monetary and fiscal policies. There are two justifications for this—political constraints and the economic crisis that began in 2008. Although it is difficult to assess how binding such constraints were, the lack of consensus in the U.S. Congress to unleash a quick support for the financial system was evident. Moreover, the lack of political agreement in the United States regarding medium-term fiscal sustainability is not only influencing the current stance of monetary policy (that is, the second round of quantitative easing) but is, in my view, one of the major threats to financial stability for the world economy.

Second, and more relevant for this discussion, the crisis justified a broader policy response than would have been called for by orthodox economic theory. Monetary and fiscal policies usually are linked in the long term by the budget constraint and should be kept separate in the medium term. However, the crisis challenged this purist approach as monetary and fiscal authorities had to assess the tradeoff between battling a banking and debt crisis or increasing indebtedness and thereby ensuring stability in the banking and monetary union. It is difficult to say when to intervene and how much is too much, but the consequences of no intervention probably would have been worse. Again, this response was relatively new to developed countries but has been the response of most emerging-market economies to financial crises, where the line between monetary and fiscal policies has been often blurred.

Despite this departure from the orthodox view, monetary and fiscal policies generally have been kept separate. The United States, United Kingdom, and European Central Bank justified intervention by noting that their charters required them to maintain the stability of the financial system and the monetary union. Moreover, expansions in their balance sheet could be perceived as temporary and should not jeopardize the long-term conduct of monetary policy. They should be able to shrink their balance sheets when conditions normalize. The perception was—and there has been some recent evidence in this direction—that the drop in asset prices was the result of extreme risk aversion and justified the intervention of monetary policy to prevent a confidence crisis.

On the fiscal front, policy focused on providing more permanent support, as occurred in the recapitalization of banks in the United States and in long-term lending to countries in macroeconomic stabilization programs in Europe. To support highly indebted countries, Europe developed the Stabilization Fund, which was funded or guaranteed by the government members. The European Central Bank's intervention in the sovereign bond market attracted criticism, but these were short-term interventions and backed by Europe's governments and should not influence the long-term conduct of monetary policy or long-term inflation expectations.

International Coordination

International cooperation remains a source of tension. During the 2008 to 2009 crisis, international cooperation improved, and the evidence was the U.S. Federal Reserve's swap lines, the International Monetary Fund programs, and the new bank regulation negotiated within the Group of Twenty countries. However, developed-market and emerging-market monetary cycles moving in opposite directions have resulted in a source of tension. The monetary-policy expansion in developed countries has resulted in excess aggregate demand in emerging markets, which has distorted local asset prices, such as exchange and interest rates.

Some have argued for more monetary-policy coordination, but it is unclear that this will happen. Unfortunately, the lack of coordination has resulted in a buildup of imbalances and more interventionist policy by countries such as China. There are no parallels in history when this has happened, and new challenges could emerge when developed central banks start compressing their balance sheets. The International Monetary Fund could play a welcome role in this area by aiming at greater coordination or at least by making countries aware of the international dimension of domestic policy choices and minimizing their side effects.

Notes

I am grateful to Dolores Palacios for expert assistance in the development of this chapter.

1. N. Batini, K. Kuttner, and D. Laxton, "Does Inflation Targeting Work in Emerging Markets?," in *World Economic Outlook*, chap. 4 (Washington, DC: International Monetary Fund, 2005).

2. International Monetary Fund, World Economic Outlook database, October 2010, www.imf.org/external/pubs/ft/weo/2010/02/weodata/index.aspx (data for Latin America and the Caribbean).

3. Irineu de Carvalho Filho, "Inflation Targeting and the Crisis: An Empirical Assessment," International Monetary Fund Working Paper 10/45 (International Monetary Fund, Washington, DC, 2010).

3

Lessons for Monetary Policy

Otmar Issing

During my time at the European Central Bank, I had a number of stimulating discussions with Olivier Blanchard, and when we disagreed—which happened from time to time—I always thought twice before continuing with my dissenting view. But he has encouraged the contributors to this volume to come up with controversial statements about the global economic crisis that began in 2008, so I have done what I would have done anyway: I examine in this chapter what I see as a flawed postcrisis consensus.[1]

Consider a statement by Lars Svensson, who is one of the gurus of the concept of inflation targeting, that shows how a strategy can be immunized against any critique: "In the end, my main conclusion so far from the crisis is that flexible inflation targeting, applied the right way and using all the information about financial factors that is relevant for the forecast of inflation and resource utilization at any horizon, remains the best-practice monetary policy before, during, and after the financial crisis."[2] According to this statement, if flexible inflation targeting has not worked as expected, either it was not applied properly or some information was missing. But the strategy was fine. In this way, you can continue with such concepts indefinitely, making mistake after mistake.

Inflation targeting was instrumental in bringing down inflation worldwide since the mid-nineties, especially in emerging countries. Some elements of inflation targeting are and should remain in consensus among all the central banks in the world—namely, the commitment to maintaining a quantitative definition of low inflation or a definition of price stability; to adopting a forward-looking policy; to presenting their views, strategy, and actions in a transparent way; and to communicating those to the markets and to the public in general. These important elements are part of inflation targeting but are also important elements in all cases in which there is no explicit inflation-targeting strategy.

One open question concerns the role of the inflation forecast. Historically, inflation targeting started with a simple concept, and its beauty was that you could look into your inflation forecast and know what to do. This was the starting point. Over time, though, the concept turned out to become more and more complicated. It soon was called *inflation targeting with judgment* and later *flexible inflation targeting*. Defining *flexible inflation targeting* as Lars Svensson has done is a nirvana approach.

One problem is that the inflation forecast is supposed to be a comprehensive summary of all elements that are relevant for inflation in the future. I doubt that this argument is valid.

Another issue concerns the time horizon of inflation targeting. At a 2003 conference at the Bank for International Settlements (BIS), inflation targeters discussed the time horizon for the inflation forecast. Initially, it was one and a half years, and then it was extended to two years. Lars Svensson asked, "Why not six or seven years?" I wonder what an inflation forecast with such a time horizon could really turn into. All concepts of inflation targeting are based on inflation forecasts in which money and credit do not play an active role. They are a passive part of the forecast but are irrelevant once it comes to monetary policy decisions.

Another issue related to time horizons is to what extent monetary policy should react to or try to deal with asset-price developments. I call this the Jackson Hole issue because it was presented at several conferences of the Federal Reserve Bank of Kansas City in Jackson Hole (e.g., 2002, 2005). Its three key points are that central banks should not target asset prices, should not prick a bubble, and should follow a mop-up strategy after a bubble has burst. I think these are all self-evident, and no central bank would act differently.

My question is always (and not only from hindsight) whether this is all. Having monetary policy dealing with asset prices only on the way down is an asymmetric approach. It implies that as long as asset prices go up, the central bank avoids responsibility. If asset prices collapse after a bubble bursts, then the central banks have to come to the rescue. I think that this asymmetric approach implies the risk of a series of ever-increasing bubbles because the causes that have led to the bubble are never corrected.

We should not repeat the mistakes of 1929 and the following years. When we are in such a situation, we have to provide the necessary liquidity. But does a totally asymmetric approach that implies a kind of guarantee from the central bank to rescue failed financial institutions not create moral hazard?

Whenever I criticize the asymmetry of this approach, I am asked how bubbles can be identified and whether central banks can know better than markets. But the issue is not identifying the appropriateness of the stock price of a company but rather assessing macroeconomic developments. A number of studies from the Bank for International Settlements and also from the European Central Bank have shown that nearly all bubbles in history have been accompanied or preceded by strong growth in money or credit.

Looking at money and credit can help the central bank to identify a risky macroeconomic situation, which leads to one of the questions that Olivier Blanchard has raised: to what extent should monetary policy contribute to containing financial instability? A major contribution would be to avoid the emergence of unsustainable developments in money and credit. But leaning against the wind might have two conceptual consequences—trying to identify asset-price misalignments and financial imbalances and leaning against unstable developments in money and credit. Both lead to the same concept.

One argument against such an approach has been that the central bank has only one instrument—the interest rate—and that this instrument is too blunt a tool to deal with asset-price developments. Interest rates would have to be raised substantially, which would create immense costs for the real economy.

But that is not a consequence of the concept of leaning against the wind. If started early enough, even small changes in the interest rate might have a substantial effect. In situations of emerging strong credit developments and unsustainable developments in asset prices, a number of financial actors typically are confronted with misalignments in maturity, so there is a maturity mismatch situation in which leveraging is going up. And changing interest rates is also a communication device that the central bank can use to signal that it cares, and it could support its communication by its publications and speeches.

With this kind of early action, it is not simple to know when to trigger. But there also is a risk in not acting soon enough. Acting early might also work against herd behavior.

As Olivier Blanchard prophetically said at the conference for my departure from the European Central Bank in 2006, "I worry that we have been lulled—or we have lulled ourselves—into a sense of complacency which is not warranted. There are still many issues we do not understand, and these may come back to bite us with a vengeance in the future." He has also noted the elegance or beauty of models, and I think this beauty has contributed to the complacency. The initial concept of inflation targeting, for example, looked elegant. In 1999, when the European Central Bank started with monetary policy, it was criticized by academics across the board who did not like its concept, which was not elegant or seen as state-of-the-art. They asked for this approach to be framed in one model, but that was not possible. There is a Nobel Prize waiting for anyone who can combine money and credit quantities with the usual concept of inflation targeting.

I think inflation targeters are aware of this issue. They are trying to include a financial sector in their model by talking about frictions. This research concept one day may lead to better approaches in the future, but for now, it does not help central banks. If the inflation-targeting approach is augmented with market frictions, what is the result? What advice can be offered to monetary policy decision makers?

I think a better answer is an approach that tries to bring in analysis of money and credit. The European Central Bank[3] called it *monetary analysis*, but from the beginning—not just from hindsight—the bank used the term for more than comparing M3 with its reference value. All aspects of monetary developments and credit were examined. This was extended over time. A book recently published by the bank demonstrates the extent of current monetary research.

We need to take other lessons from the global economic crisis. For me, dealing with the zero bound for interest rates by raising the inflation target is not a convincing approach for several reasons. Blanchard and his colleagues have dealt with the costs of inflation and have argued in favor of indexing the tax system, but this is difficult to implement and is not as efficient as stable money.[4]

But my main concern is the unavoidable loss of credibility of the central bank. Why should people believe that an upper limit of, for example, 4 percent inflation would not be increased again next time? How can inflation expectations be anchored with such an approach? The widening of the range would increase volatility. It would foster short-term activism. Finally, more leeway for reducing interest rates might be required than is needed with a smaller range. But this aspect of the problem has to be discussed further.

This debate also leads to the issue of dual versus single mandate. No central bank in the world would ignore developments in the real sector, such as unemployment. But what the central banks can deliver in the end is price stability and nothing else. Responsibility for financial stability finally is in the hands of regulatory and supervisory authorities.

Price stability and financial stability must not be seen as a tradeoff. Financial stability must be dealt with in the context of monetary policy that is geared to maintain price stability.

Notes

1. For a deeper analysis see Otmar Issing, "Lessons for Monetary Policy: What Should the Consensus Be?," IMF Working Paper 11/97 (International Monetary Fund, Washington, DC, 2011).

2. Lars E.O. Svensson, "Flexible Inflation Targeting: Lessons from the Financial Crisis" (The Netherlands Bank, Amsterdam, September 21, 2009).

3. European Central Bank, "Enhancing Monetary Analysis" (Frankfurt, 2010).

4. Olivier Blanchard et al., "Rethinking Macroeconomic Policy," *Journal of Money, Credit, and Banking* 42, no. 26 (2010).

4

Macroeconomics, Monetary Policy, and the Crisis

Joseph Stiglitz

I begin with a simple observation: the current global economic crisis was man-made. This was the consensus of both the U.S. Financial Crisis Inquiry Commission in its 2011 report,[1] as well as a broad range of economists. The economic crisis that began in 2008 in the United States was not inevitable. The implication is that policies, particularly the policies of the U.S. monetary and regulatory authorities, led to the crisis. (In many countries, central banks have responsibilities as regulatory authorities and, I think, should have such obligations.)

Sins of both commission and omission—most notably, excessive deregulation, a failure to effectively enforce the regulations that existed, and the failure to adopt new regulations reflecting changes in financial markets—made the economies of the United States and, to some extent, Europe vulnerable to collapse. These failures led to the crisis and have continued in its wake.

The economies in the United States and Europe have been brought back from the brink where they stood in September 2008 but have yet to be brought back to robust growth. Some policies, like the second round of U.S. quantitative easing (QE2), may have even contributed to instability in the global economy. They are also having adverse effects on global financial integration.

This crisis was caused by excesses in credit markets, which led to the creation of a bubble. This is not the first time that excesses in credit markets have led to bubbles that break and lead to a recession. For the past two hundred years, severe economic crises have been associated with finance, with excess credit expansions, the creation of bubbles, and the breaking of those bubbles. (Carmen M. Reinhart and Kenneth S. Rogoff have documented the long history of such crises in their 2009 book, *This Time Is Different: Eight Centuries of Financial Folly,* and even before that, so did Charles Kindleberger.[2]) The 1990 recession in the United States was related to the collapse of many savings and loan institutions, and the financial sector played a central role in the 1997 East Asia crisis.

How Flawed Models Contributed to the Crisis and Provided Inadequate Guidance on How to Respond

In the aftermath of the 2008 crisis, there has been much debate about whether to blame the financial markets (which failed to allocate capital well and mismanaged risk) or the regulators (who failed to stop the markets' misbehavior). But economists (and their models) also bear responsibility for the crisis. Flawed monetary and regulatory policies were guided by economists' models, and the dominant models failed to predict the crisis and said that such a crisis could not or would not happen. Even after the bubble broke, those relying on such models said that the effects would be contained. In most models, the disturbances to the tranquility of the economy were exogenous, but historically—as now—the important shocks are endogenous.

One of the reasons for the failures of these models was their inadequate modeling of credit markets (banks and shadow banks). If this were the first time that a credit boom and bust had caused a major downturn, one could say that the profession had developed models that worked most of the time and that this was an unusual event. But these recurrent crises have shown that the failure of mainstream monetary and macroeconomics to analyze credit markets—and ways to reduce the risk of disorderly expansions and contractions—is among the central failures of monetary economics in recent decades. Even today, this lacuna has its effects, for in spite of the mega-bailout, credit flows have not been restored to, for example, small and medium enterprises (SMEs), and the mortgage securitization market remains broken. Years after the breaking of the bubble, the government is still underwriting a large fraction of all mortgages. The standard macro and monetary policies have provided little guidance, and to the extent that they have given guidance, it has evidently been deficient.

The Importance of the Right Microfoundations

In the aftermath of what has been called the "new classical" revolution,[3] there was a consensus that macroeconomics should be put on sound microfoundations. The big mistake was that some economists put it on the wrong microfoundations. They turned to the microfoundations of competitive equilibrium analysis—an approach that, at the time that it became the foundation for the new macroeconomics, was being undermined by several strands of research, including work in game theory and on the economics of imperfect and asymmetric information. The standard competitive model was particularly suspect for an analysis of macroeconomics because it assumed full employment and its assumptions were the singular set of assumptions under which markets, by themselves, work well.

The emerging consensus (based in part on historical experience but also based in part on theoretical work on the economics of imperfect and asymmetric information and incomplete risk markets), which has been reflected in much of the discussion (and Guillermo Ortiz, who was a student of mine at Stanford, mentions this in chapter 2), is that markets by themselves are not always efficient. Whenever markets have imperfect information and incomplete risk, the markets are almost never efficient. They are also not stable, and this crisis is one of the worst manifestations of problems that have been recurrent.

The Key Missing Element: Credit

As I have noted, a key missing element in the standard models is credit. In normal times, money and credit are highly correlated, so we can use one for the other. But crises are not normal times, and the relationship between money and credit breaks down in such times. It is precisely at such times that reduced-form relationships, such as between money and credit or money and GDP, are no longer useful, and may actually be very misleading. One then has to return to structural models, focusing on the links between what the central banks do and the flow of credit. This aspect should have been at the center of modeling and of policy. What has come to be called the "Lucas critique"[4] emphasized the importance of structural models for the analysis of the consequences of policy changes because of the effect of those policy changes on expectations. But the standard models were ad hoc and not structural in the postulated relationships involving money (for instance, in the relationship between money and GDP), with even more profound implications for both prediction and policy.

Some have defended these lacunae in the same way that some defend the Fed's not taking preemptive action to contain the bubble. The claim is made that before the crisis, no one saw the bubble coming, and, so too, no one before the crisis recognized these deficiencies in the standard model. But neither defense has much merit. There were many who warned forcefully of the bubble, explaining with some precision what was going on and what the consequences of the breaking of the bubble would be. But if one is wedded to a model that says that markets are efficient and bubbles don't occur, then there is little reason to heed such warnings. So too, there was a large literature on the relationship between credit and macroeconomic activity; or more accurately, I should say that there were large *literatures,* because there were many traditions— including a Latin American tradition, an older microeconomic tradition, and a newer microeconomic tradition that was derived from the economics of information, focused on the role of credit markets in ascertaining creditworthiness and designing and enforcing credit contracts in the presence of information asymmetries.[5] None of these many traditions were incorporated into mainstream macroeconomics.

Here I focus on three issues—objectives and targets, instruments, and governance. I conclude by returning to the role of modeling in providing insights into these and other key policy issues.

Objectives of Monetary Policy

The crisis has brought home something that should have been recognized even before the crisis: managing inflation is not an end in itself but a means to an end. The end is a more stable economy—not just price stability but real stability—and an economy that is growing faster in a sustainable way. We ought to be concerned about how the economy affects ordinary individuals. And here, employment and wages are critical.

The perspective that low and stable inflation leads to a stable real economy and fast economic growth was never supported by either economic theory or evidence, and yet it became a main tenet of central-bank doctrine. This idea has been destroyed by the crisis—and it ought to have been. Economists focused on the *n*th-order social losses that arise from disequilibrium relative prices that arise in the presence of inflation, on the deadweight loss of consumer surplus that results when price misalignments occur. Focusing on inflation diverted attention away from something that was much more important, the far larger, first-order consequences of financial instability. Indeed, the price misalignments were not even of second-order importance. They were more like tenth order of significance relative to the losses resulting from the failure of the financial market. With the output gap, those losses have reached trillions of dollars. Compared to that, the losses in the consumer surplus that come from the small microeconomic misallocations are miniscule. The crisis has shown that financial stability is far more important than price stability.

The idea that targeting inflation will lead to financial stability or that focusing on only price and financial stability is sufficient for maintaining a low output gap and stable and robust growth is fundamentally flawed. (In extreme cases, of course, where the issue is not 3, 4, or 5 percent inflation but more like 10 percent inflation, central banks must focus on inflation as well. But in places like the United States and Europe, where inflation has been controlled, this is not the issue.)

Instruments

What instruments are at our disposal? Some central bankers claimed that they had only one instrument, the interest rate, and that it was a blunt instrument. Even, granted, that there was a bubble (which the standard models said could not occur), it was claimed that were they to have tried to contain it by raising interest rates, there would have been severe adverse effects, sending the economy into a downturn. But monetary authorities and regulatory authorities have a wide range of instruments, and the interest rate is only one instrument that affects the flow of credit and aggregate demand and aggregate supply. The constraint that they not use these other instruments was self-imposed, perhaps because they believed too much in the models that said that the economy was efficient. There were, in particular, a wide range of regulatory measures that could and should have been taken and that would have at least dampened the bubble and thus lessened the severity of the consequences of its breaking. Indeed, Congress had explicitly given the Fed additional regulatory authority in 1994.

Macroprudential Regulation

It has long been recognized—*outside of what before the crisis had become the conventional wisdom, supported by the "standard model"*—that macroprudential regulation is needed to stabilize the economy. Such regulation can take a variety of forms, including provisioning requirements and cyclically adjusted capital adequacy requirements, and so forth. Indeed, it was even recognized that capital adequacy requirements that were not cyclically adjusted, especially with mark-to-market accounting, could be destabilizing (acting as an automatic *destabilizer*).

Monetary policy affects the economy not just (or even so much) through the interest rate but also through credit availability. Credit availability is of first-order importance and is especially affected by such regulations. But such regulations also affect the interest rates at which banks lend, and, if economic activity is affected by the interest rate, it is that interest rate, as much as (or even more than) the T-bill rate that matters.

The Spread

One of the important endogenous variables in the macroeconomic system is the lending rate. The relationship between the U.S. Treasury bill rate and the lending rate can change over the cycle. It can change in different circumstances, and modeling that spread ought to have been an essential part of the modeling of monetary models. But most models did not include it—and therefore had nothing to say about how policy might affect it.

Leverage

An essential aspect of financial-sector regulation concerns restrictions on leverage. Policy discussions that require banks to have more capital often seem to begin with the presumption that there are benefits to more leverage, which have to be weighed against the costs, but the discussions of the presumptive benefits of leverage ignore the insights provided by Franco Modigliani and Merton Miller.[6] The Modigliani-Miller theorem[7] argues that corporate financial structure doesn't matter—changes in leverage or debt equity ratios don't affect the total value of the firm. Increasing leverage shifts risks around. And if banks benefit, it is largely either because shareholders don't understand the risks they face or because they do—they realize that by increasing leverage, they are getting the government to absorb more of the downside risk, in the inevitable bailouts that follow. Many economists (including myself) have noted problems with the Modigliani-Miller theorem at the microeconomic level (for instance, information may be conveyed by corporate financial structure). But at the macroeconomic level, the basic insight of Modigliani and Miller—that more leverage does not mean a more efficient use of capital—remains persuasive. Increased leverage means that equity becomes riskier. With banks that are too big to fail, increased leverage increases the likelihood of a bailout.

The Second Round of Quantitative Easing (QE2)

In this crisis, monetary authorities have increasingly made use of an instrument that previously was seldom used—buying long-term bonds (long-term government bonds, or even mortgages). This has come to be called "quantitative easing." This policy reflects a focus on the interest rate as the key economic instrument in current macroeconomic/monetary policy in the United States. With short-term interest rates already as low as they could go, attention naturally shifted to what monetary authorities could do about long-term interest rates. The second round of quantitative easing (QE2) has been defended on the grounds that it will lower the long-term interest rate and that lower long-term interest rates will stimulate the economy. Most people around the world feel that QE2 has led to a flood of liquidity, which has not helped the country that needs liquidity—the United States—but rather has caused enormous disturbances in booming emerging markets, which do not need additional liquidity. This is not a surprise.

The main channel by which monetary policy normally affects the economy is the credit channel, and the credit channel, especially to small and medium enterprises, is still blocked. (Many of the regional and community banks that traditionally do a disproportionate share of SME lending are still weak; and much of the lending is collateral-based, and the value of the collateral— typically real estate—has greatly diminished with the crash.) Larger enterprises, awash with cash and with excess capacity, were not likely to invest more simply because long-term interest rates were slightly lower. To the extent that more credit was made available, markets looked for where returns were highest and risk lowest—in the booming emerging markets, not the moribund U.S. economy. Money is going where it's not wanted and not going where it's needed.

Lowering interest rates may lead to higher asset prices, helping to fuel another asset bubble. The monetary authorities should have been cautious about doing so, given the repeated problems that such asset bubbles have presented for the economy.

The Fed welcomed the increase in equity and bond prices that lower interest rates might bring about, suggesting that it would encourage consumption. The significance of these effects, however, may be more limited than its advocates claim, since the intervention has been announced to be temporary. If the government's purchase of bonds leads to higher prices for stocks and bonds, its later sales should lead to a lower price. If markets anticipate this, then knowing that in the future prices will be lower limits the rise of the prices today. If there are significant effects, they arise out of market imperfections, which typically are not well modeled. But if market imperfections are significant enough to imply a significant effect on prices today, the boost to consumption of such temporary increases in prices will be limited. And there are two significant adverse effects. First, there will be large potential losses by the central bank. The fact that the central bank does not use mark-to-market accounting does not make these losses any less real. Second, the attempt to hide the losses (to ensure that they are not recognized) may impede the conduct of monetary policy.

That relates to one of the critiques of the first round of quantitative easing (QE1). Basically, it temporarily lowered long-term interest rates. With private parties recognizing that they would experience a capital loss on any long-term mortgage, it was unattractive for any private party to engage in the mortgage market. In that way, it destroyed the private mortgage market. As the low interest rates (particularly in the U.S. context, with no prepayment penalties) pushed people to refinance their mortgages, the mortgages moved off the banks' balance sheets onto the government's books. The banks were effectively bailed out, as the risk of these assets becoming nonperforming was moved off their balance sheets. This was an important hidden part of the bailout.

There is one channel through which quantitative easing may have had some effect: it may have led to an exchange rate that was lower than it otherwise would have been. In effect, the United States was engaged in competitive devaluation.

The Assignment Problem

A standard part of the conventional wisdom is that there should be as many instruments as there are objectives, with each instrument assigned to an objective. Thus, monetary policy—interest rates—is assigned to the objective of price stability. But it is a mistake to think that different instruments and objectives can be assigned to different agencies to allocate responsibility neatly, with each agency having one instrument and one objective. All instruments have to be coordinated. The Nash equilibrium that would emerge from an uncoordinated system, with each agency assigned one instrument and pursuing its own objective, will generally not be efficient. In the presence of uncertainty, even with a single objective, it will in general be desirable to use multiple instruments.

Governance

While the theory of monetary policy in recent years has largely been shaped by macroeconomic models, which I have suggested were badly flawed, how monetary policy has been conducted has largely been shaped by a set of beliefs about what constitutes good institutional structures. Attention in and outside the IMF has focused on governance, on the structure of decision-making institutions and the incentives (implicit and explicit) facing decision makers. The conventional wisdom argued for independent central banks. But the independent central banks did not perform better—and in many instances they performed much worse—in the run-up to the crisis. The crisis should, accordingly, make us rethink our ideas about so-called good governance, just as it should lead to a rethinking of the underlying models.

The notion of independence of central banks raises questions of accountability. Central banks reflect certain parties' perspectives, particularly those of the financial markets. When Alan Greenspan said that he was surprised that banks did not look after their risk better, I was surprised that he was surprised. Any microeconomist looking at the incentives that were in place would have said that the banks had incentives for excessive risk taking and shortsighted behavior. The repeal of the Glass-Steagall Act led to the formation of much-too-big banks that were too big to fail. Again, incentive structures encouraged excessive risk taking. We would have had to rewrite our microeconomics textbooks if we had *not* had a crisis. Greenspan evidently was taken in by the views prevailing in the financial sector that ignored problems posed by agency issues and externalities. With central banks accountable largely to financial markets, it was not surprising that there was "cognitive capture." That is, they have been seduced by ideas that prevailed in the financial sector, even if these ideas did not serve the national interests well.

Not only was there a failure by the Fed to take actions that would have prevented, or at least lessened, the crisis, how it responded to the crisis also reflected its cognitive capture. I have come to have views close to those of Simon Johnson, who used to be the chief economist at the IMF. When we saw this crisis coming, we both feared that there would be a massive redistribution of wealth in the wrong direction, and there was. We feared that there would be a lack of transparency, and there was. (The AIG bailout has become emblematic of both.)

One can have independence, but it must be independence with representativeness, and that is where we have failed.[8]

Modeling

The central thesis of this chapter is that economists' models did not describe or reflect what was really going on before, during, and after the crisis. Our models of macroeconomics did not include agency problems or the risk-taking decisions of banks. What is especially remarkable is that central banks had models in which banking did not play an important role. In their own self-interest, they should have tried to make banking important. And banking *is* important, even though their models did not capture this.

There were also deeper mathematical flaws in the structure of the models: they embedded assumptions of concavity, which meant risk diversification necessarily worked. But whenever a crisis emerges, contagion is mentioned, and the natural mathematical assumptions in analyzing contagion are different. Integration worsens problems of contagion. Coherent models, consistent with both views of the world, both before and after the crisis, were never developed, at least among those in the mainstream.

Moving forward, the challenges for modeling will be great. But many of the building blocks have existed for a long time. There are good models of banking, good models of the risks of excessive interconnectivity within the financial sector, good models of credit bubbles, good models of agency problems. Because those building blocks were not considered before the last crisis, the insights into policy that they provided were given short shrift, as, for instance, banks were allowed to become too interconnected and to be too self-regulated. At the same time, we failed to connect central banking to the rest of our society—and the rest of economics.

Notes

1. The Financial Crisis Inquiry Commission, *The Financial Crisis Inquiry Commission Report: Final Report of the National Commission on the Causes of the Financial and Economic Crisis in the United States*, 2011, http://fcic-static.law .stanford.edu/cdn_media/fcic-reports/fcic_final_report_full.pdf (accessed September 20, 2011).

2. C. P. Kindleberger, *Manias, Panics, and Crashes: A History of Financial Crises* (New York: Basic Books, 1978).

3. Lucas's 1972 paper is often cited as the seminal work in new classical economics. See R. Lucas, Jr., "Expectations and the Neutrality of Money," *Journal of Economic Theory* 4, no. 2 (1972): 103–124. See B. Greenwald and J. E. Stiglitz, "Keynesian, New Keynesian, and New Classical Economics," *Oxford Economic Papers* 39, no. 1 (1987): 119–133, for a more extended analysis of the importance of providing the right microfoundations.

4. Robert Lucas, Jr., "Econometric Policy Evaluation: A Critique," in *Carnegie-Rochester Conference Series on Public Policy*, vol. 1, ed. K. Brunner and A. Meltzer (New York: Elsevier, 1976), 19–46.

5. See, in particular, my book with Bruce Greenwald, *Towards a New Paradigm in Monetary Economics* (Cambridge: Cambridge University Press, 2003).

6. In the aftermath of the crisis, this point seems at last to have begun to be grasped. See, for example, the U.S. Senate Committee on Banking, Housing, and Urban Affairs hearing, "Debt Financing in the Domestic Financial Sector," August 3, 2011, including my testimony and the references cited there.

7. See F. Modigliani and M. Miller, "The Cost of Capital, Corporation Finance, and the Theory of Investment," *American Economic Review* 48, no. 3 (1958): 261–297. They later showed that dividend policy also was irrelevant, in "Dividend Policy, Growth, and the Valuation of Shares," *Journal of Business* 34, no. 4 (1961): 411–433. I subsequently generalized these results (in J. E. Stiglitz, "On the Irrelevance of Corporate Financial Policy," *American Economic Review* 64, no. 6 [1974]: 851–866) while at the same time showing the limitations imposed by bankruptcy and information asymmetries. See also J. E. Stiglitz, "A Re-Examination of the Modigliani-Miller Theorem," *American Economic Review* 59, no. 5 (1969): 784–793; and J. E. Stiglitz, "Information and Capital Markets," in *Financial Economics: Essays in Honor of Paul Cootner*, ed. William F. Sharpe and Cathryn Cootner (Englewood Cliffs, N.J.: Prentice Hall, 1982), 118–158. For a broader discussion, see J. E. Stiglitz, *The Selected Works of Joseph E. Stiglitz*, vol. 2 (Oxford: Oxford University Press, forthcoming).

8. In 2011, U.S. congressman Barney Frank introduced legislation to make the Federal Reserve more representative.

II

Fiscal Policy

Questions: How Should the Crisis Affect Our Views of Fiscal Policy?

The issues involving fiscal policy that are raised by the global economic crisis fall largely into two categories. One set of issues concerns the use of fiscal policy for short-run stabilization, and the other involves the long run. Of course, many issues involve interactions between short-run and long-run considerations.

Fiscal Policy as a Tool of Stabilization Policy

Before the crisis, there was broad consensus that monetary policy should be the primary tool of stabilization policy and that fiscal policy should play little role beyond allowing automatic stabilizers to operate. But almost all major countries used discretionary fiscal policy during the crisis. This raises a host of issues:

1. Was it appropriate to use discretionary fiscal policy? If so, is this because exceptional circumstances made this appropriate, or should discretionary fiscal policy become a regular part of the stabilization toolkit?

2. Should automatic stabilizers be strengthened, and if so, how? Should institutional changes be made to increase the flexibility of discretionary fiscal policy, and if so, what should they be?

3. How dependent are the effects of fiscal policy on the circumstances under which it is used? For example, the effects might depend on whether monetary policy is constrained by the zero lower bound, on whether the financial system is functioning well, on whether the government's long-run fiscal situation is sound, and on whether the economy is weak or strong. Are there circumstances when stimulus can jump-start a weak economy? That is, can it move the economy to a path of robust growth,

or is it better to think of stimulus as merely filling in gaps left by private demand?

4. How large are the effects of various kinds of fiscal stimulus? Has the crisis provided significant new evidence about those effects? Should discretionary fiscal stimulus rely more on measures that affect intertemporal incentives (temporary sales tax holidays and investment incentives, phased-in increases in value-added taxes, and so on) and rely less on broad tax cuts and increases in transfers and government purchases?

5. What have we learned about the political economy of fiscal stabilization? Does the political backlash mean that overwhelming force needs to be used in designing stimulus?

6. Should mechanisms be in place to promote international cooperation in discretionary fiscal policy and to ensure that the international spillovers are considered in designing fiscal stimulus?

7. How large are the budgetary costs of fiscal stimulus in a weak economy? What about the argument that if hysteresis is present, a fiscal stimulus can actually pay for itself?

8. With many economies still facing both extended periods of weakness and looming long-run fiscal problems, what is the right timing of the switch from expansionary fiscal policy to combat the crisis to fiscal consolidation to address the long-run fiscal challenges? What should determine the timing and speed of the switch?

The Unsustainable Long-Run Fiscal Trajectory

Before the crisis, fiscal policy in many countries was already on a long-run trajectory that was not sustainable. The loss of revenues from the crisis and (to a smaller extent) the discretionary fiscal response have brought that long run considerably closer. Again, this raises numerous issues:

1. To what extent did dismal long-run fiscal outlooks constrain the short-run responses to the crisis?

2. How should the crisis change our views about the debt-to-GDP ratios that countries should aim for in the long run? On the one hand, the events of recent years show the value of having the fiscal space to respond

to a crisis. On the other, the deterioration of fiscal positions because of the crisis makes it harder to achieve a given debt-to-GDP ratio.

3. Can immediate fiscal consolidation be expansionary in the short run? At one extreme is the view that permanent consolidation is often expansionary, particularly if it is done on the spending side. At the other extreme is the view that it is expansionary only when there is imminent danger of a sovereign debt crisis. Similarly, how large are the potential expansionary effects of back-loaded fiscal consolidation, such as announcements of future increases in the retirement age (which would be expected to reduce life-cycle saving) and announcements of phased-in increases in value-added taxes (which create incentives for consuming sooner rather than later)?

4. How soon do various countries need to take steps to address their long-run fiscal challenges? What fiscal rules, if any, have proved useful in the past in actually reducing deficits and returning debt to a sustainable path?

5. How should countries and international institutions (such as the International Monetary Fund and the European Central Bank) respond to stresses placed on countries by high interest rates on their sovereign debt? How should they respond to full-blown sovereign debt crises?

6. There is a wide range of possible ways of dealing with long-run budget challenges, such as enacting broad-based increases in income or consumption taxes, broadening the tax base, putting caps on discretionary spending, raising the retirement age, and passing various types of reforms to pension and health-care systems. What general principles should guide countries in their decisions about the mixes of the various options they should use?

7. Is there a need for fundamental institutional reform in fiscal policy? How should we think of fiscal rules in the context of a common currency area, such as the euro zone? What about such proposals as e-bonds or allowing euro countries access to multilateral financing conditional on strong fiscal policy?

5

Fiscal Stimuli and Consolidation

Parthasarathi Shome

Developed and emerging countries alike introduced fiscal stimuli in response to the global financial crisis of 2008. Affected countries experienced severe economic contraction—reduction in or negative growth in gross domestic product. This was generally accompanied by a decline in revenue per GDP and a rise in expenditures per GDP. The revival of economic activity anchored on quantitative easing did not materialize because the injected money, M, did not move to improve m, the collapsed money multipliers. The focus turned to fiscal stimuli through tax reductions and mainly current expenditure enhancements. But the size of the fiscal multiplier was not known either. The dilemma was whether the same fiscal stimuli would work to the same extent across countries. The already rising fiscal deficit per GDP was further exacerbated, and public debt per GDP in some countries almost doubled. Stock markets and rating agencies did not appreciate the direction of these indicators, and strategies had to be reformulated.

Strategies were refocused on fiscal consolidation, although its pace was debated. One view was that fiscal loosening should continue, another was that fiscal policy should be tightened, and a third view was to go somewhere in between. Elections were won and lost on this issue. In the United Kingdom, for example, preelection (March 2010) and postelection (June) positions viewed corrective policies very differently. Further, the final spending review (October) recomposed expenditure components in favor of investment over consumption, cutting back on untargeted direct consumption subsidies and reducing the length and pattern of unemployment coverage. Thus the choice made was one in favor of rapid consolidation through lower consumption, in contrast to the earlier demand-driven (consumption plus investment) strategy. In India's

February 2011 annual budget of the central government, fiscal consolidation is shown to be taking place through economic growth and from the expenditure side. Tax revenue will grow in real terms but not through any net discretionary measures. Thus, though both countries are taking fiscal consolidation measures, a single pattern does not emerge.

The difficulty with using fiscal multipliers has been demonstrated convincingly by Ethan Ilzetzki, Enrique G. Mendoza, and Carlos A. Végh (2010). They show that the effect of fiscal stimulus depends on the particular characteristics of an economy. Larger fiscal multipliers result from higher-income countries, less open economies, fixed rather than flexible exchange-rate regimes, lower public debt, and higher investment than consumption (figure 5.1).[1] The implication is that the same fiscal deficit per GDP will lead to different stimuli in different countries, which poses a formidable challenge to using fiscal deficit per GDP as an indicator for reining in contagion globally.

Small and medium-sized banks and credit channels (and their borrowers) did not receive the benefit of stimuli. There was also a psychological

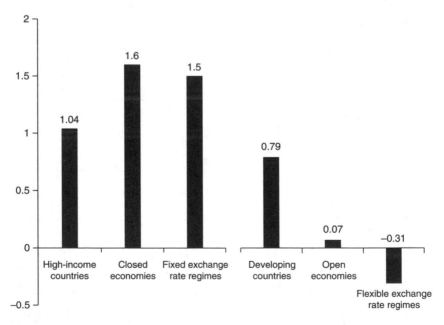

Figure 5.1
Estimated values of fiscal multipliers. *Source:* Ilzetzki, Mendoza, and Végh (2010).

phenomenon or barrier for banks to lend, reflecting the overall uncertain environment with subprime loans. In any event, recognition of that problem led to a refocusing on fiscal multipliers, and then to a kind of dilemma with the usefulness of fiscal multipliers. To assess what countries actually did, I examined India and the United Kingdom, two countries with relatively extreme economic indicators in terms of per-capita GDP and economic growth rates, to see if any lessons could be drawn for fiscal coordination internationally.

In 2010, the United Kingdom had a preelection budget in March, the general election took place in May, there was a postelection budget in June, and a spending review firmed up the final consolidation picture in October. The exercise was carried out for a period of projections up to 2014–2015 and in some aspects up to 2015–2016. The process (1) increased taxes, (2) maintained investment spending, (3) scaled back current spending considerably, and (4) within current spending, cut back benefits (direct subsidies) much more than public services such as the National Health Service. The right combination emerged among (1) tax and expenditure, (2) investment and current spending, and (3) pure consumption and service-oriented current spending (table 5.1).

This new fiscal policy mix relied more on spending cuts than on tax increases and was in line with the findings of academicians such as Alberto Alesina and Silvia Ardagna (2009), who found that fiscal adjustments mostly on the spending side are better suited for avoiding large recessions. Further, the projections for the rise in public debt per GDP were scaled back by almost five percentage points by 2014–2015. Preelection campaigning revealed the overall direction of fiscal tightening that the Conservatives planned as postelection policy, and they nevertheless won. This appeared to justify a finding by Alberto Alesina, Roberto Perotti, and José Taveres (1998) that fiscal rectitude was rewarded by voters. In general, it appears that governments, when backed into a corner, tend to take appropriate fiscal measures. This happened in the United Kingdom, despite a considerable reduction in projections for the economic growth trajectory.[2] In addition, because the nominal fiscal tightening of the postelection government is larger than that of the preelection one, the fiscal consolidation turns out to be even more stringent in terms of (the lowered) GDP.

Table 5.1
United Kingdom: Selected indicators, 2010 to 2014

	2010	2012	2014
*Real GDP growth**			
March budget 2010	1.25%	3.5%	3.25%
June budget 2010	1.2	2.8	2.7
October 2010 spending review[a]	1.8	2.6	2.8
*Public-sector net borrowing (as percentage of GDP)**			
March budget 2010	11.1	6.8	4
June budget 2010	10.1	5.5	2.1
October 2010 spending review[a]	10	5.6	1.9
*Cyclically adjusted surplus on current borrowing (as percentage of GDP)**			
March budget 2010	-4.6	-2.5	-1.3
June budget 2010	-4.8	-1.9	0.3
October 2010 spending review[a]	-4.7	-1.8	0.5
*Net public debt (as percentage of GDP)**			
March budget 2010	63.6	73	74.9
June budget 2010	61.9	69.8	69.4
October 2010 spending review[a]	60.8	69.1	68.8
Total tightening (billions of pounds), of which	72.4	112.6	110.3
Spending per tax (ratio)	70/30	74/26	73/27
Current per investment spending (ratio)	66/34	77/23	79/21

Notes: a. Economic data taken from Office of Budget Responsibility, "Economic and Fiscal Outlook" (Autumn 2010); * Figure given for tax years (that is, 2010 = 2010/11).

In India's 2011/12 central budget, which was presented in Parliament on February 28, 2011, fiscal consolidation of 1½ percent of GDP has come from the expenditure side (table 5.2). Of this, ½ percent is from cutbacks in subsidies alone (see table 5.2). These moments offer an excellent opportunity to correct structural deficiencies in expenditure. Just as the United Kingdom recomposed its expenditure, what India seems to be doing postcrisis is scaling back distortionary subsidies on fertilizers, food, and petroleum, while during the crisis it loosened its fiscal stance, including on subsidies (table 5.3). Announcements of cutbacks in subsidies have not affected elections adversely so far.

There was no net revenue generation through discretionary tax measures in the budget, but India is anticipating two major structural tax reforms in both income and consumption taxes, prior to which the

Table 5.2
India: Fiscal consolidation, 2008 to 2012

	2008–2009	2009–2010	2010–2011	2011–2012 Budget
	(Δ% to GDP)			
1. Tax revenue (net to center)	-0.87	-0.97	0.19	0.24
2. Nontax revenue	-0.32	0.04	1.02	-1.40
3. Capital receipts[a]	-0.76	0.39	-0.10	0.21
4. Total consolidation of revenue side	-1.95	-0.55	1.10	-0.94
	(Δ% to GDP) × -1			
5. Nonplan expenditure	-0.72	-0.10	0.58	1.34
6. Plan expenditure	-0.82	0.30	-0.38	0.10
7. Total consolidation of expenditure side	-1.54	0.19	0.20	1.44
8. Fiscal deficit (7 + 4)	-3.5	-0.4	1.3	0.5
9. Primary deficit	-3.5	2.9	1.1	0.4

Notes: + indicates tightening; - indicates loosening. a. Does not include receipts in respect of market stabilization scheme and excludes borrowings and other liabilities.

Table 5.3
India: Tightening of subsidies

	2008–2009	2009–2010	2010–2011	2011–2012 Budget
	(Δ% to GDP) × -1			
Subsidies, of which	-0.92	0.17	0.07	0.49
Fertilizer	-0.76	0.44	0.24	0.14
Food	-0.15	-0.11	0.12	0.09
Petroleum	0.01	-0.18	-0.26	0.22
Interest	-0.01	0.02	-0.03	-0.01
Other	-0.01	-0.01	0.00	0.04

Note: + indicates tightening; - indicates loosening.

government appears not to be taking major discretionary action. There is widespread anticipation that the tax structure will be rationalized and that uncertainties that are embedded in the structure will be reduced. In sum, when tax and expenditure are consolidated in the fiscal sector, the numbers reveal a clear pattern of relaxation during the crisis followed by quick tightening postcrisis. On the whole, India has selected a countercyclical fiscal path, although it is not a mirror image of the policy mix selected by the United Kingdom.

I conclude, therefore, that stakeholders in society need massive fiscal stimuli only extraordinarily. They have become mature and trust rational fiscal policies that do not generate inequity through untargeted subsidies or burden them through generations. Voters will reward sensible fiscal policy. Further, since the size of fiscal multipliers varies across countries, reflecting their particular characteristics, fiscal deficit per GDP of each country will produce a different stimulus. Thus, a country with a low fiscal multiplier would need to be accommodated with a higher fiscal deficit before any international action is triggered, compared with one that has a higher fiscal multiplier. It is therefore not feasible to fix a single fiscal deficit per GDP as a trigger for an internationally driven domestic-policy change.

Instead, the International Monetary Fund, with its recently enhanced resources, should seek the sanction to take stronger action in contagion countries based on each country's own fiscal performance in a historical or time-series perspective rather than on the basis of a cross-country perspective. Flexibility for the Fund in that intervention should be safeguarded, and its strength buttressed with stronger nonstatic analysis in the Fund's regular financial programming framework.

When it is understood that, for containing or averting global financial contagion, it is best to deemphasize traditional indicators and triggers spanning real, monetary, fiscal, and external sectors, it should be possible to develop meaningful ones to contain financial contagion. A few traditional indicators—based on current-account imbalances, the size and movement of foreign-exchange reserves, and external (particularly short-term) debt—would continue to have to be used. But the challenge remains to design indicators targeting financial instability more directly. These would be based on, among others, potential flight capital, volatility of capital flows and stock markets, and interest-rate spreads that tend to precede or are associated with financial crises. Empirical evidence does exist. Basel II was not successful, and Basel III has moved part of the way (Shome and Rathinam 2010). What is needed is the resolve of developed economies and the leadership from multilateral institutions, particularly the Fund, which should push for such sharpened indicators rather than broad ones.

Notes

1. The fact that high-income countries generally are also open economies with flexible exchange rates does not detract from the overall argument that fiscal multipliers are likely to be different across economies.
2. The new projections were much closer to the average of the projections made by the main independent projectors.

References

Alesina, Alberto, Roberto Perotti, and José Tavares. 1998. "The Political Economy of Fiscal Adjustments." *Brookings Papers on Economic Activity* 29:197–266.

Alesina, Alberto F., and Silvia Ardagna. 2009. "Large Changes in Fiscal Policy: Taxes versus Spending." National Bureau of Economic Research Working Paper 15438, National Bureau of Economic Research, Cambridge, MA.

Ilzetzki, Ethan, Enrique G. Mendoza, and Carlos A. Végh. 2010. "How Big (Small?) Are Fiscal Multipliers?" National Bureau of Economic Research Working Paper 16479.

Shome, Parthasarathi, and Francis Xavier Rathinam. 2010. "India's Expectations from G20." *Global Financial Stability: A Dialogue on Regulation and Cooperation.* Bonn: Deutsche Gesellschaft für Internationale Zusammenarbeit (GIZ) GmbH. Shorter version at http://www.voxeu.org/index.php?q=node/6127.

6

What Have We Learned about Fiscal Policy from the Crisis?

David Romer

The financial and macroeconomic crisis that began in 2008 has shattered some of the core beliefs of macroeconomists and macroeconomic policymakers:

- We thought we had macroeconomic fluctuations well under control, but they are back with a vengeance.
- We thought that the zero lower bound on nominal interest rates was a minor issue, but it has proved central to the behavior of the macroeconomy.
- We had not paid much attention to issues of financial regulation and financial disruptions, but they too have turned out to be critical to macroeconomic performance.
- The idea that policymakers would tolerate years of exceptionally high unemployment due to a deficiency of aggregate demand has gone from unthinkable five years ago to fact today.
- The workhorse new Keynesian dynamic stochastic general equilibrium (DSGE) models on which we were concentrating so much of our attention have been of minimal value in addressing the greatest macroeconomic crisis in three-quarters of a century.

In short, we have a lot of reflection to do. In this chapter, I focus on four lessons about fiscal policy that I think can be learned from the crisis.[1]

Lesson 1: We Need Fiscal Tools for Short-Run Stabilization

The first lesson is straightforward: we need fiscal tools for short-run stabilization. Before the crisis, there was broad agreement among macroeconomists and policymakers that short-run stabilization was almost exclusively the province of monetary policy. Monetary policy is more flexible, more easily insulated from political pressures, and more easily placed in the hands of independent experts. We thought that the zero lower bound would bind infrequently and not sharply—and that in the unlikely event that it did bind sharply, monetary policymakers had other tools to use in place of reductions in the policy interest rate.[2]

We now know that this view was wrong. We suffered shocks larger than what almost anyone thought was within the realm of reasonable possibility. The constraint imposed by the zero lower bound turned out to be huge (for example, Rudebusch 2009). And central banks did not use tools other than the policy rate on a scale even remotely close to large enough to make up for the loss of stimulus caused by the zero lower bound.

Perhaps the lack of aggressiveness in using those tools reflects an understanding of the costs of using them that has eluded conventional analyses. But central bankers have yet to provide evidence of such costs. A more likely possibility is that the culture of central banking makes it much easier to take unusual steps when the financial system is at risk than when the threat is "merely" years of exceptionally high unemployment. But regardless of the reason, monetary policy was not used aggressively enough to prevent very large demand shortfalls.

Countries needed other tools, and the alternative to monetary tools is fiscal ones. For that reason, almost every major country adopted substantial discretionary fiscal stimulus in the crisis (U.S. Council of Economic Advisers 2009). Since there could be another major demand shortfall in the future, it follows that instruments of discretionary fiscal stimulus are needed as part of the macroeconomic toolkit.

Lesson 2: We Have Even Stronger Evidence That Fiscal Policy Is Effective Than We Did before the Crisis

In a major crisis, the demand shortfall is likely to be large and long-lasting. Moreover, the possibilities for policies that shift intertemporal incentives are limited. As a result, much of discretionary fiscal stimulus is likely to take largely conventional forms, such as broad-based income tax cuts, increased transfers, and higher government purchases. The second lesson is that the evidence that has come out of the crisis has made it even clearer that such conventional fiscal actions stimulate the macroeconomy.

As Robert Solow has noted (see chapter 8, this volume), we should not be trying to find *the* multiplier: the effects of fiscal policy are highly regime dependent. One critical issue is the monetary regime. Consider estimating the effects of fiscal policy over the period from, say, 1985 to 2005. Central banks were actively trying to offset other forces affecting the economy, and they had the tools to do so. If they were successful, the estimated effects of fiscal policy would be close to zero. But this tells us nothing about the effects of fiscal policy in situations where monetary policymakers are unable or unwilling to offset other forces.

Fortunately, the crisis has sparked a great deal of work on the short-run effects of fiscal policy, much of it focusing on settings where monetary policy does not respond aggressively. Some of it uses evidence from the crisis itself, but much does not; some focuses on a particular country, usually the United States, but some uses larger samples; and a considerable body of the work looks at evidence from different regions within a country, again usually the United States. One particularly appealing aspect of this last set of studies is that because monetary policy is conducted at the national level, it is inherently being held constant when one is looking at within-country variation.

Collectively, this research points very strongly (although not unanimously) to the conclusion that when monetary policy does not respond, conventional fiscal stimulus is quite effective.[3] And a careful examination of the evidence gives no support to the view that when monetary policy is constrained, fiscal contractions are expansionary (International Monetary Fund 2010).

Even so, I find even more compelling two types of evidence that predate the crisis. The first comes from wars. The major increases in government purchases in the two world wars and the Korean War were associated with booms in economic activity, and those booms occurred despite very large tax increases and extensive microeconomic interventions whose purpose was to restrict private demand. These outcomes appear to be overwhelming evidence that fiscal stimulus matters.

The other type of evidence is more general evidence about the functioning of the macroeconomy. We know that monetary policy has powerful real effects (which means that aggregate demand matters), that current disposable income is important to consumption, and that cash flow and sales have strong effects on investment.[4] It would take a strange combination of circumstances for those things to be true but for fiscal policy, which one would expect to work through those channels, not to be effective.

Given this wide range of evidence—not to mention the large body of precrisis work on the effects of fiscal policy that I have not touched on—I think we should view the question of whether fiscal stimulus is effective as settled.

Lesson 3: Fiscal Space Is Valuable

The third lesson is that fiscal space is valuable. That is, being in a healthy fiscal situation is important to responding aggressively to a collapse of demand.

One way to see the value of fiscal space is by considering a thought experiment. Suppose that the United States or the countries of Europe had begun the crisis with a modest debt-to-GDP ratio, no looming entitlement problems, and confidence that policymakers would not let a temporary stimulus become permanent. It is hard to think of any strong force that would have prevented policymakers from enacting much more fiscal stimulus than they did. In the United States, for example, there might have been a much larger personal tax cut, a large one-year or two-year payroll tax holiday, and perhaps twice as much relief for state and local governments. My guess is that the stimulus would have been closer to $1.5 trillion than to the $0.8 trillion that was actually enacted. The result would have been a milder downturn and a much faster recovery.

The other way to see the importance of fiscal space is to look at countries that had it. Without examining the evidence systematically, I am reluctant to draw firm conclusions. But China, Korea, and Australia, which have sound fiscal situations, undertook relatively large fiscal expansions even though they were not hit exceptionally hard by the downturn and still had considerable room to spare on monetary policy. And Iceland, which entered the crisis with little debt, undertook policies that raised its debt-to-GDP ratio by about 100 percentage points.

Thus, aggressive fiscal stimulus can greatly reduce the costs of a macroeconomic crisis, but lack of fiscal space can greatly constrain stimulus. It follows that having fiscal room to maneuver is valuable.

Lesson 4: Political Economy Considerations Are Extremely Important

The fourth and final lesson has a different character. It is that in understanding fiscal policy responses to the crisis, political economy considerations are central.

It is not hard to describe some of the major features of the most appropriate fiscal response to the crisis. A very large short-run stimulus would have been coupled with the enactment of measures that yielded very large improvements in the long-run fiscal outlook over time. The timing of the actual long-run tightening would have been tied to monetary policy exit: only when monetary policymakers would otherwise have raised interest rates would the fiscal tightening begin. Some measures would have simultaneously addressed both the short-run and long-run problems. An example is phased-in increases in value-added taxes, which act like reductions in real interest rates and generate revenue over time. And policy would have been incremental: some measures would have been enacted in response to the beginnings of the crisis, and then they would have been expanded or contracted if the crisis proved more or less severe than expected.

This description does not fit actual policy well. With few exceptions, countries did not adopt substantial back-loaded fiscal contraction together with a short-run stimulus. The scale of the stimulus was far less than what could have been done if it had been coupled with major long-run consolidation. Measures that simultaneously addressed short-run and long-run problems were rare. And the response to the fact that the crisis proved far worse than almost everyone originally thought was not to increase stimulus commensurately. Indeed, in many cases it was to cut back on stimulus.

The source of the large gap between actual policies and those I have described as most appropriate is not sophisticated analyses suggesting that the policies that have been pursued are better. Rather, the source is in the workings of political systems.

Both theory and evidence indicate that the reasons that the political process often leads to highly undesirable outcomes are not to be found in models of rational agents with sophisticated economic understandings who have the misfortune of being caught in games whose equilibria are highly inefficient. Rather, they are to be found in the simple fact that voters' incentives to understand difficult policy issues are minimal. As a result, they—understandably—rely on intuition, superficial impressions, and emotion in their political decisions (Caplan 2007; Romer 2003).

In the case of fiscal stimulus in response to a massive downturn, I think that economists grossly overestimated our success in conveying basic macroeconomic messages about the value of government budget deficits when private demand collapses. When the crisis came, those messages were swept away by voters' gut feeling that when ordinary people are suffering and have no choice but to cut back, then for the government to be profligate is not just unwise but morally offensive. Likewise, although there are large benefits to enacting policies that gradually address long-run budget problems, those benefits are not enough to overcome the barriers created by the fact that few citizens know much about the specifics of the long-run fiscal outlook, and so react negatively to concrete plans to cut spending or raise taxes relative to current policy—even though maintaining current policy is not feasible.

Where Does This Leave Us?

I think that these lessons leave struggling countries and concerned policymakers in pretty bad shape. We face both a severe short-run problem and a severe and closely related long-run one.

In the short run, the crisis is still going on. In the advanced economies, resource utilization remains deeply depressed relative to normal, with no prospect of rapid recovery. In the United States, the likelihood is a painfully slow return to normal; in much of Europe and in Japan, there are few signs of any return at all. Having a conference about "policies in the wake of the crisis" today strikes me as a little like having a conference on the lessons from the Great Depression in 1934.[5] Now is not the time for a contemplative look back; it is time for redoubled efforts to figure out what can be done and to make it happen.

Sadly, the prospects do not appear good. It is still easy to characterize what should be done. In the advanced economies, there should be aggressive use of creative monetary policy, short-run fiscal stimulus, and measures to address the long-run fiscal problems. But the political environment is skeptical of monetary actions, hostile to fiscal stimulus, and only a shade more open to long-run fiscal consolidation than it usually is. Unfortunately, I do not have anything better to propose to economists than that we not resign ourselves to years of high unemployment when it is curable, and that we make the case over and over again for policies that will bring about improvement.

The related long-run problem is that we may face another crisis sometime in the next several decades. The Great Depression led to institutional changes—deposit insurance, financial regulation, and attention to stabilization policy—that made a recurrence less likely. Nothing as significant appears to be coming out of the current crisis. There has been some financial regulatory reform around the world, but how effective it will be is not yet clear. The political environment may make it harder in future crises to use the extraordinary monetary, financial, and fiscal tools that kept this crisis from spiraling completely out of control. And the crisis has worsened countries' long-run fiscal problems. This both reduces the fiscal space that would be available in the event of a future crisis and increases the chances that a crisis will start through a loss of confidence in countries' fiscal soundness.

Again, I see no easy solutions. Economists can continue to make the case for the value of the types of policies that were followed in the crisis. We can argue for reforms that will make the financial system more resilient. We can make the case for reforms that will strengthen the fiscal response to a crisis, such as automatic triggers for some types of fiscal policy changes and putting some aspects of discretionary fiscal policy in independent, expert hands. And we can explain the need for long-run consolidation.

I think we should make those arguments as frequently and as forcefully as possible. But I do not see deep grounds for optimism that we will be heard.

Notes

I am grateful to Christina Romer for helpful comments. The views expressed are purely my own.
1. My claim about DSGE models is not directly about fiscal policy and so is not covered in this chapter, but it may require some elaboration. I am not asserting that modern macroeconomics in general has not been valuable. To give just one example, empirical and theoretical work on credit-market imperfections (for

example, Bernanke 1983; Bernanke and Gertler 1989; Kiyotaki and Moore 1997) offers important insights into financial crises and very likely informed the policy response. However, the real-time performance of the models that represented the precrisis state of the art of the new Keynesian DSGE research program was dismal (Edge and Gürkaynak 2010). And most insights from the extensions of those models in response to the crisis arise more transparently in models that dispense with much of the new Keynesian DSGE superstructure. Caballero (2010) provides a broad critique of the workhorse models.

2. Reifschneider and Williams (2000) provide a representative example of an analysis suggesting the likely unimportance of the zero lower bound. Eggertsson and Woodford (2003) and Svensson (2003) discuss alternative tools. Bernanke (2000, 2002) argues forcefully that even in the presence of the zero lower bound, monetary policy could be relied on to prevent deflation—and, by extension, an extended period of abnormally low inflation and weak real performance.

3. For within-country evidence, see Chodorow-Reich, Feiveson, Liscow, and Woolston (2011); Suárez Serrato and Wingender (2011); Shoag (2010); Fishback and Kachanovskaya (2010); and Nakamura and Steinsson (2011). For cross-country evidence, see International Monetary Fund (2010); U.S. Council of Economic Advisers (2009); and Kraay (2011). For time-series evidence (as well as simulation-based evidence), see Hall (2009); Barro and Redlick (2011); Fisher and Peters (2010); Coenen et al. (2010); and Christiano, Eichenbaum, and Rebelo (2011). On this list, all but Kraay, Barro and Redlick, and Fisher and Peters implicitly or explicitly try to provide evidence about the case where monetary policy does not act to offset the effects of fiscal policy. With the exception of two of these three, all the papers suggest substantial effects of fiscal policy (the two exceptions are Kraay and Barro and Redlick, which suggest moderate effects). As I describe below, this brief tour omits all work that predates the crisis.

4. The literature on departures from the permanent-income hypothesis is much too voluminous to summarize here. One important point is that much of the evidence of departures comes from countercyclical changes in taxes and similar interventions, and so is directly relevant to fiscal policy. One recent example is Parker, Souleles, Johnson, and McClelland (2011). My own summary of work on cash flow and investment can be found in Romer (2012, 447–451). For sales and investment, see, for example, Abel and Blanchard (1986).

5. I was tempted to ask who chose the conference title until I remembered that I was one of the organizers. In our defense, it seemed like a better idea in 2009 than it does now.

References

Abel, Andrew B., and Olivier J. Blanchard. 1986. "The Present Value of Profits and Cyclical Movements in Investment." *Econometrica* 54 (March):249–273.

Barro, Robert J., and Charles J. Redlick. 2011. "Macroeconomic Effects from Government Purchases and Taxes." *Quarterly Journal of Economics* 126 (February):51–102.

Bernanke, Ben S. 1983. "Nonmonetary Effects of the Financial Crisis in the Propagation of the Great Depression." *American Economic Review* 73 (June):257–276.

Bernanke, Ben S. 2000. "Japanese Monetary Policy: A Case of Self-Induced Paralysis?" In *Japan's Financial Crisis and Its Parallels to U.S. Experience*, ed. Ryoichi Mikitani and Adam S. Posen, 149–166. Washington, DC: Institute for International Economics.

Bernanke, Ben S. 2002. "Deflation: Making Sure 'It' Doesn't Happen Here." Remarks before the National Economists Club, Washington, DC, November.

Bernanke, Ben S., and Mark Gertler. 1989. "Agency Costs, Net Worth, and Business Fluctuations." *American Economic Review* 79 (March):14–31.

Caballero, Ricardo J. 2010. "Macroeconomics after the Crisis: Time to Deal with the Pretense-of-Knowledge Syndrome." *Journal of Economic Perspectives* 24 (Fall):85–102.

Caplan, Bryan. 2007. *The Myth of the Rational Voter: Why Democracies Choose Bad Policies*. Princeton: Princeton University Press.

Chodorow-Reich, Gabriel, Laura Feiveson, Zachary Liscow, and William Gui Woolston. 2011. "Does State Fiscal Relief during Recessions Increase Employment? Evidence from the American Recovery and Reinvestment Act." Unpublished paper, August.

Christiano, Lawrence, Martin Eichenbaum, and Sergio Rebelo. 2011. "When Is the Government Spending Multiplier Large?" *Journal of Political Economy* 119 (February):78–121.

Coenen, Günter, et al. 2010. "Effects of Fiscal Stimulus in Structural Models." International Monetary Fund Working Paper WP/10/73, International Monetary Fund, Washington, DC, March.

Edge, Rochelle M., and Refet S. Gürkaynak. 2010. "How Useful Are Estimated DSGE Model Forecasts for Central Bankers?" *Brookings Papers on Economic Activity* 2:209–244.

Eggertsson, Gauti, and Michael Woodford. 2003. "The Zero Bound on Interest Rates and Optimal Monetary Policy." *Brookings Papers on Economic Activity* 1:139–233.

Fishback, Price V., and Valentina Kachanovskaya. 2010. "In Search of the Multiplier for Federal Spending in the States during the New Deal." National Bureau of Economic Research Working Paper No. 16561, National Bureau of Economic Research, Cambridge, MA, November.

Fisher, Jonas D. M., and Ryan Peters. 2010. "Using Stock Returns to Identify Government Spending Shocks." *Economic Journal* 120 (May):414–436.

Hall, Robert E. 2009. "By How Much Does GDP Rise If the Government Buys More Output?" *Brookings Papers on Economic Activity* 2:183–231.

International Monetary Fund. 2010. "Will It Hurt? Macroeconomic Effects of Fiscal Consolidation." *World Economic Outlook*, chap. 3. Washington, DC: International Monetary Fund.

Kiyotaki, Nobuhiro, and John Moore. 1997. "Credit Cycles." *Journal of Political Economy* 105 (April):211–248.

Kraay, Aart. 2011. "How Large Is the Government Spending Multiplier? Evidence from World Bank Lending." Unpublished paper, World Bank, June. *Quarterly Journal of Economics*, forthcoming.

Nakamura, Emi, and Jón Steinsson. 2011. "Fiscal Stimulus in a Monetary Union: Evidence from U.S. Regions." National Bureau of Economic Research Working Paper No. 17391, National Bureau of Economic Research, Cambridge, MA, September.

Parker, Jonathan A., Nicholas S. Souleles, David S. Johnson, and Robert McClelland. 2011. "Consumer Spending and the Economic Stimulus Payments of 2008." National Bureau of Economic Research Working Paper No. 16684, National Bureau of Economic Research, Cambridge, MA, January.

Reifschneider, David L., and John C. Williams. 2000. "Three Lessons for Monetary Policy in a Low-Inflation Era." *Journal of Money, Credit and Banking* 32 (November, pt. 2):936–966.

Romer, David. 2003. "Misconceptions and Political Outcomes." *Economic Journal* 113 (January):1–20.

Romer, David. 2012. *Advanced Macroeconomics.* 4th ed. New York: McGraw-Hill.

Rudebusch, Glenn D. 2009. "The Fed's Monetary Policy Response to the Current Crisis." *Federal Reserve Bank of San Francisco Economic Letter* No. 2009-17, May.

Shoag, Daniel. 2010. "The Impact of Government Spending Shocks: Evidence on the Multiplier from State Pension Plan Returns." Unpublished paper, Harvard University, Cambridge, MA.

Suárez Serrato, Juan Carlos, and Philippe Wingender. 2011. "Estimating Local Fiscal Multipliers." Unpublished paper, University of California, Berkeley, March.

Svensson, Lars E. O. 2003. "Escaping from a Liquidity Trap and Deflation: The Foolproof Way and Others." *Journal of Economic Perspectives* 17 (Fall): 145–166.

U.S. Council of Economic Advisers. 2009. "The Effects of Fiscal Stimulus: A Cross-Country Perspective." Washington, DC, September.

7

Fiscal Policy Responses to Economic Crisis: Perspectives from an Emerging Market

Sri Mulyani Indrawati

This chapter focuses on fiscal policy responses to the global economic crisis of 2008 from the perspective of an emerging-market country, drawing on my experience as minister of finance of Indonesia at that time.

Crises Past and Present

For emerging economies, the 2008 global economic crisis was markedly different from previous crises of the 1980s and 1990s. Most of those economic crises were the result of policy or institutional problems in the emerging-market countries themselves. These problems included bad macroeconomic policy, bad governance, or weak institutions that led to instability, low growth, high inflation, credit collapse, and balance-of-payments problems.

The first decade of the new millennium, in contrast, was characterized by the investment of many developing countries in strengthening their own policies, including adopting more sound macroeconomic policies. Many of the central banks in developing and emerging countries became more independent. They adopted inflation targeting. Fiscal policy became more prudent. Some countries even adopted a fiscal cap, which in Indonesia's case prohibited the fiscal deficit from exceeding 3 percent of gross domestic product in any single fiscal year. Indonesia also adopted a cap on its debt-to-GDP ratio, prohibiting it from exceeding 60 percent. Most important, many developing countries also invested in structural reforms, both on the revenue and expenditure sides but also in investment and trade policy.

This investment in structural reforms in the last three decades has meant that many developing countries have developed macroeconomic and fiscal space, including significant external reserves. These buffers further strengthened economic growth and stability. However, this stronger domestic performance did not prevent emerging markets from being exposed to external shocks, particularly when efforts had also been made to open up to trade and foreign investment and to integrate into the global economy.

The 2008 crisis was thus different from crises of the past for most developing countries. The source of the shock was external, coming from the global economy and from problems that had their inception in more advanced countries. What affected developing countries most from this crisis was the sense of a global collapse in confidence, particularly in financial markets. The market ceased to work. There was no liquidity. There ceased to be transactions across banks, even in Indonesia. There was no trust among banks. There was a real and imminent threat to the banking system, whose intermediary function was not working. The capital outflow from emerging countries that ensued during this crisis (in an irrational flight to "quality") further aggravated the situation of the domestic banking and financial system in emerging markets. So there was a collapse not only in external demand but also in domestic demand.

Policy Levers in Managing the Crisis

What were the options for developing-country policymakers to restore confidence in the financial system while stimulating demand? With regard to financial-sector measures, with a collapse in markets, we resorted to some unconventional measures to restore liquidity and confidence. As finance minister, I used my discretion to move government funds out of the government accounts at the central bank and into state-owned banks, instructing them to channel this liquidity into the commercial banking system. Even then, given the lack of confidence across these market segments, the funds were slow in traveling through the financial system. Other Asian countries adopted a blanket guarantee on bank credit. In addition, we delayed implementing mark-to-market accounting for government bonds held by banks and mutual funds. Again, this measure was taken to get transactions going again and to help restore confidence to banks so that they would reenter into transactions.

For emerging economies, the most critical policy lever for addressing the collapse in external and internal demand was to resort to fiscal policy. Fiscal policy—on both the revenue and expenditure sides—was critical in helping countries deal with this recent crisis.

First, a key consideration in deploying fiscal policy in this crisis was to choose policies that would immediately affect the economy. This meant identifying policies that are fast to generate demand and that are fast to enact, involving fewer administrative and political processes for implementation. One could opt for a one-time tax facility, whether an income tax reduction, a reduced value-added tax for a year, or a reduced import tariff for raw materials. An example of an expenditure policy that immediately stimulates demand is cash transfers, since these immediately affect disposable income and also help protect the poor, who are usually severely affected by economic crises.

One way to make the fiscal policy response faster is to put into place automatic stabilizers, even if temporary. In Indonesia's 2009 budget, it was agreed that the government would be allowed discretion for increased fiscal spending should economic indicators deteriorate further than agreed parameters. The government was authorized to increase spending to "stabilize" the economy, particularly to help protect employment and the poor, for example, if a further banking crisis occurred or if inflation was higher than expected. Providing this discretion to government to react flexibly with fiscal policy in midyear in the case of crisis makes the political process for policy adjustment more expedient. The political concern and consensus were such that government was given this authority.

Second, as noted above, a high priority for fiscal policy during economic crises are programs that protect the poor and can support employment generation or cushion income during these times. Social-protection programs such as cash-transfer programs are useful in this regard, particularly because they are generally better targeted than commodity subsidies. Social-protection programs that include workfare or food for work might also be prioritized.

Third, thinking ahead is important, and spending must be maintained on those items that will strategically support future recovery and growth. Many developing countries are still underinvested in infrastructure for growth. Investing in development expenditure, such as on infrastructure, which stimulates employment while positioning the country for future growth, should be a priority for fiscal stimulus programs during crises.

The Role of International Cooperation

International cooperation can play an important role during global crises, particularly when market confidence is an issue. During the height of the economic crisis of 2008, there was intense dialog among global leaders and finance ministers. The coordinated action and unified view taken by the leaders of the Group of Twenty at the time (2008 to 2009), first in Washington and then in London, provided a strong boost to confidence. Coordinated action at the time was also facilitated by a common diagnostic of the source and ramifications of the problems that were affecting all countries, as well as the convergence in policy actions that would be needed to address the crisis (that is, expansionary fiscal and monetary policies to counter the weakening economies). Currently, international coordination is more challenging and complicated because countries or regions are at different stages of crisis or recovery, requiring different policy directions and solutions.

There is also a role for international responses during crises in the area of financing. As noted, even with sound policies, during the global economic crisis, international financial markets were thin and even irrationally skittish, leading to high risk premia. Emerging-market economies, which were trying appropriately to undertake fiscal stimulus packages to get domestic and global demand going again, were having a hard time entering the market to raise deficit financing. In the case of Indonesia, for example, the World Bank issued what it called a "deferred draw-down option" (a contingent financing vehicle), which was of great help. This kind of support helps allow a developing country to speak with confidence in the market. It signals that the international community views the fiscal stance as appropriate. It enables developing countries to avoid paying an unreasonable interest rate, especially when the market behaves irrationally.

Challenges for Fiscal Policy in the Wake of the Crisis

The main challenge for fiscal policy in the wake of the crisis is determining the timing, sequencing, and strategies for fiscal consolidation. In designing the path for consolidation, sequencing is important. In particular, restoring confidence and securing the structural reforms necessary to cement and anchor that confidence are critical before a country starts cutting spending. In addition, timing is also dictated by the nature of the external environment and shocks. In the case of this global economic crisis, even if the signs of recovery are anemic, policymakers are appropriately concerned about other uncertainties in the external environment. Today these include escalating commodity prices (including food and fuel), instability in the Middle East, and sovereign debt crises. In addition, partly owing to the weak global recovery, many emerging markets have been trying to cope with rapid capital inflows, which create complications in terms of asset bubbles and inflationary pressures. The timing and sequencing of fiscal consolidation have to account for this dynamic external environment, which poses multiple threats, while focusing on the fundamentals of each country's domestic economic structure.

Regarding strategies for fiscal consolidation among developing-country economies, several aspects need to be stressed. First, many developing countries have a narrow tax base. For them, a priority for structural reform is to broaden the tax base, improve revenue, and put into place an automatic stabilizer that covers the majority of the real economy. Second, countries should cap discretionary spending, which also creates better fiscal discipline. This also avoids politicizing discretionary fiscal policy during a crisis. Third, countries need to focus on improving the quality of their spending, which becomes essential during a crisis. Prioritizing spending in areas such as the social sectors and infrastructure might be key, as well as ensuring that spending is well targeted.

Conclusion

These are some insights and lessons learned from the perspective of an emerging-market country policymaker who struggled, along with colleagues, to manage the global economic crisis. The perspective of developing countries in handling such a global crisis may be somewhat different from that of advanced economies. But the recent economic crisis has shown that today's global economy is ever more interconnected. It pays to come together to address international economic contagion and to learn from others' experiences.

8
Fiscal Policy

Robert Solow

One important lesson that I hope we have learned from the global economic crisis that began in 2008 and the deep recession that has followed is that economies like that of the United States can experience uncomfortably long intervals of general excess supply or excess demand. Economists and interested civilians used to know this. But it was largely forgotten during the great moderation during the two decades leading up to the crisis and the accompanying optimism among economists and civilians about smoothly self-correcting markets.

The general belief then was that monetary policy was an adequate tool for taking care of minor blips. During long and deep recessions, however, it has become evident that monetary policy may reach its limits without being able to generate enough aggregate demand to close the excess supply gap. So governments have turned more or less instinctively to discretionary fiscal policy, even if the latest refined theory cannot approve. If we are going to do discretionary fiscal policy, we should try to do it right.

The usual way to calculate the likely effects of fiscal policy—meaning increases in particular government expenditures and particular decreases in particular tax rates—is through the use of estimated multipliers. The trouble is that existing estimates of those multipliers tend to vary widely, from negative numbers to substantial positive numbers. This does not inspire confidence. We have to understand why the range is this wide and then find acceptable ways to narrow it. Those who disapprove of discretionary fiscal policy tend to find smaller multipliers, and those who approve tend to find larger ones. But this tendency can be turned into healthy criticism and lead, if not to consensus, then to a narrower range.

One useful starting point is the easy realization that multiplier values depend on the state of the economy and also on the character of other economic policies at the time. Here are three examples. Any econometric estimate of *the* multiplier has to notice that there may be two-way causality between aggregate output and public expenditure. So it is natural to search for exogenous public expenditures as a basis for estimation. An obvious candidate is military spending. The trouble is that large increases in military spending often come at times when the economy is already using essentially all of its capacity to produce. But then the real-output multiplier must be essentially zero. All that military spending can do is to displace other spending. The estimation of fiscal-policy multipliers should be confined to observations on an economy with a substantial margin of excess supply. When that is done, the picture changes. Robert Gordon and Robert Krenn (2010) have recently given a striking example. War production and preparation for war had already eaten up much excess capacity in the United States by the end of 1941. If a government-spending multiplier is estimated from time series through mid-1941, a number near 2 emerges. If the same analysis is carried through the end of 1941, the estimated multiplier is near 1.

The second example has attracted a lot of attention recently and has to do with monetary policy. Suppose that the central bank follows a standard Taylor rule. Then monetary policy functions like an automatic stabilizer. The rule tells the central bank to offset, at least partially, any increase in real GDP, even if the economy is currently weak. (One may wonder whether this is sensible, and I come back to this question.) The size of the apparent fiscal-policy multiplier depends on the strength of the central bank's offsetting reaction. It has been pointed out that, in a deep recession like the present one, the rule may want the central bank's policy rate to be negative. When that rate has reached its lower bound of zero, there is nothing further to do. The Taylor rule is suspended. But a fiscal-policy-induced increase in real output may leave the target rate still negative, in which case the rule-following central bank will not change its policy rate and thus will not oppose the increase in output. So multipliers should be larger when the zero lower bound on the policy rate is effective, and this has been found, by Robert Hall among others, to be empirically the case.

A third example turns on the proportion of any policy-induced increase in disposable income that is likely to be saved. There is evidence that, when the burden of household debt is high, even relatively poor households tend to use windfalls to pay down debt. This is a form of precautionary saving and reduces the size of the multiplier. Smart fiscal policy takes this into account and adjusts accordingly.

This suggests that a new round of more economically sophisticated estimates might narrow the range of expected multiplier effects and improve the making of discretionary fiscal policy.

I mentioned in passing that monetary policy, if conducted according to a Taylor rule, functions like an automatic stabilizer. The advantages of automatic stabilizers are fairly obvious. Bypassing the legislative process can shorten the lag in policy response to an adverse shock and probably scale the fiscal response better to the size of the need. In the American context, it may avoid some of the partisan stupidities inside and outside Congress that drive serious students up the wall.

There are disadvantages, however. One is that there are no "neutral" taxes or spending programs, so that automatic stabilizers have unintended effects on allocation and distribution. This makes them hard to legislate in the first place and may make them unpopular in operation.

Another disadvantage is the one mentioned in connection with the Taylor rule. Automatic stabilizers are intended to dampen economic fluctuations. They do this generally by partially offsetting both upward and downward movements of, say, real output. When output peaks and starts to fall, we welcome a force that works against the downswing (unless there is large excess demand). But when output reaches bottom and starts to rise, we are less happy with a force that slows the recovery. But that is the way most automatic stabilizers work, from the Taylor rule to unemployment insurance.

An earlier literature tried to deal with this problem through a slightly more complicated approach called *formula flexibility*. A simple proportional tax system is already an automatic stabilizer in both directions. One can imagine a tax system in which the whole collection of rates is a function of the Okun gap and its rate of change. On paper, such a system could encourage any movements toward the target output and resist movements away from it. (A Taylor rule could be similarly refined.)

Formula flexibility tries to mimic what intelligent discretionary policy would do. If it could be legislated once and for all, with adjustment only at intervals, that could be a gain. But it is hard to imagine it being legislated at all.

I conclude with brief comments on two other issues. The expansion of world trade and capital flows implies that there is need for international coordination of fiscal policy, whether discretionary or automatic. Especially in Europe, but in principle everywhere, the cross-border leakages are now large enough that free riding on one side encourages reluctance to act on the other. Unfortunately, the prevalence of spillovers is especially complicating for automatic stabilization, which ought in principle to be tied partially to international economic conditions, although conducted nationally.

Finally, discretionary fiscal-policy moves need to be better targeted than they have been in the United States. This refers both to longer-run need and to short-term effectiveness. I am thinking of such devices as focused investment tax credits, perhaps time-limited, as an alternative to across-the-board income tax reductions. Aiming at infrastructure is difficult in an economy with low public investment generally because infrastructure projects are harder to start than to accelerate efficiently, which is hard enough. In economies and labor forces that are more and more service-oriented, public spending aimed at job creation should look more at the efficient production of needed services. Again thinking of my own country, urban amenity might be a good place to start. I am sure I can leave it to others to point out that countercyclical fiscal policy can leave long-term hangovers of debt that need credible planning immediately and actual fixing in due course.

Reference

Gordon, Robert J., and Robert Krenn. 2010. "The End of the Great Depression 1939–41: Policy Contributions and Fiscal Multipliers." National Bureau of Economic Research Working Paper 16380, National Bureau of Economic Research, Cambridge, MA. http://www.nber.org/papers/w16380.

III

Financial Intermediation and Regulation

Questions: How Should the Crisis Affect Our Views about Financial Intermediation and Regulation?

The financial sector, which until 2008 had been hailed as a hub of innovation and a driver of growth, led to a crisis that brought the world economy to the brink of collapse and caused unemployment for millions. As a result, there is broad agreement on the need for reform that minimizes the chances of future catastrophes while maintaining as much as possible of the social benefits of the financial sector. Unfortunately, there is little agreement beyond that. The range of issues concerning financial intermediation that policymakers must consider is exceptionally wide.

Whose Fault: Markets or Governments?

One set of issues concerns the role of government in laying the groundwork for the crisis. In one view, the financial system is inherently prone to instability, and the key failure of policy was excessive deregulation and faith in laissez-faire. But another view is that the roots of the crisis stem from excessive government involvement. The usual suspects here are implicit government guarantees (of institutions that are too big to fail and of various assets that are not formally guaranteed by the government). Other suspects are deposit insurance, with its attendant reduction in incentives for private monitoring, and government efforts to steer credit in particular directions.

Many views are more nuanced. For example, some basic types of government involvement (such as insuring small depositors and bailing out institutions whose imminent collapse threatens enormous disruptions) are arguably either clearly desirable on economic grounds or inevitable on political ones. If those involvements are taken as given, preventing them from generating adverse consequences (through moral hazard, for example) may require additional regulation.

Determining the sources of financial crises and the interactions of government involvement and private drivers of instability is thus a crucial step in deciding how to move forward.

The Social Value of the Financial Sector?

Another basic issue that must be addressed before policymakers can decide how to treat the financial sector is its economic importance. At one end of the spectrum is the view that the sector has enormous social value by channeling saving to productive uses and spreading risk. At the other end is the view that much of what happens in the sector consists of rent seeking (for example, arbitraging away mispricings that would otherwise be arbitraged away a few milliseconds later).

The social value of the financial sector's activities obviously has important implications for how it should be regulated. For example, the lower its social value, the stronger the case for slowing financial innovation and deregulation to the point where regulators can minimize the chances that they are creating macroeconomic risk.

How Active Should Regulation and Supervision Be?

It is appealing to think that we can greatly increase stability by building substantial shock absorbers into the system. Most notably, substantial capital requirements both increase the size of the shocks needed to push institutions into insolvency and better align private and social incentives. Downpayment requirements for mortgages and margin requirements for purchases of equity can play similar roles. But this view may be too facile. In a world of sophisticated financial instruments, arbitrarily large risks can be held on arbitrarily small balance sheets. Thus there may be an inherent need for more active supervision and regulation. And presumably, there are social costs to shock absorbers (otherwise, why not have 100 percent capital requirements, 100 percent downpayment requirements, and so on?), so there is a case to be made that regulators should monitor the tradeoffs between the costs and benefits and adjust the regulations in response. In short, the issue of comparatively passive versus comparatively active regulation is another critical one.

How to Design Capital-Market Institutions?

Shock absorbers and supervision are not the only tools of regulation. A different approach is to try to change the institutions of capital markets to improve incentives. Examples include greater emphasis on long-term compensation, greater roles for shareholders and boards of directors, transactions taxes, and taxes on leverage or debt. Policymakers need to better understand the tradeoffs among shock absorbers, supervision, and institutional reform, and the costs and benefits of various types of institutional changes.

How to Mitigate the Effects of Crises?

Another set of reforms considers ways not to reduce the risk of crises but to mitigate their effects when they occur. Examples include resolution authority for insolvent financial firms (for which traditional bankruptcy does not work well), requirements that some or all of the debt issued by financial firms convert to equity in a crisis, and requirements that financial firms purchase some type of crisis insurance. In designing such policies, policymakers must consider both their likely effectiveness in a crisis and how they would affect the performance of the system in normal times and the likelihood of a crisis developing. Unfortunately, knowledge about these subjects is limited; thus they too are important and pressing topics.

How Limited Is Our Understanding?

The final and perhaps most fundamental challenge in designing reforms of the financial system is a lack of agreement about the appropriate conceptual framework. In the case of pollution, for example, there may be disagreement about the specifics, but there is a clear framework underlying the case for government involvement: pollution involves negative externalities and so can be addressed by such tools as Pigouvian taxes and the auctioning of tradable permits. In the case of financial markets and financial failures, in contrast, analysis tends to operate at the level of metaphor (for example, credit is the lifeblood of the economy), analyses of particular markets and institutions, and specific models whose generality is unclear. A requirement for being able to confidently design appropriate financial regulation is a clear understanding of the market failures that warrant intervention—which is something that we do not currently have.

9

Financial Crisis and Financial Intermediation: Asking Different Questions

Y. V. Reddy

The financial sector, which once was hailed as the driver of growth, brought about a global crisis in finance and the real economy in 2008. Reforms are needed in the financial sector and also in the ways that we think about the financial sector in the context of the ultimate objectives of economic and social well-being.

Rather than asking the same questions that were asked before the crisis and getting the same answers, we need to ask a different set of questions or put the same questions differently. This chapter examines India's experience with regulation of the financial sector.

Financial-sector reforms need to minimize the chances of future catastrophes and yet maintain as many as possible of the social benefits of the financial sector. Is there merit in considering, more seriously than is the case now, the experiences of other countries with the crisis? The financial crisis originated in some countries with great intensity, but its intensity in the financial sector varied among countries. One question is whether it is appropriate to universalize the causes of crisis on the basis of the most affected countries (such as the United States) or whether it would be better to analyze the variations in the intensity of the financial crisis in different countries (say, Canada, Australia, China, or India). In November 2007, the *Economist* identified India, Hungary, and Turkey as the most vulnerable economies among the emerging-market economies, but in two of the three countries its prediction proved to be wrong. Was the framework for assessment of vulnerability wrong? Similarly, inflation targeting helped in obtaining credibility for policies and thus price stability. But in many countries, price stability was maintained without inflation targeting. The question is whether countries that achieved credibility through inflation targeting can now give up the instrumentality of inflation targeting, retain a focus on price stability, and acquire operational flexibility to maintain some output and financial stability.

How should the reform agenda of the financial sector be linked to other policies? Precautionary steps may be taken in the regulation of the financial sector to reduce the risks that may emanate from other policies. The regulatory framework for the financial sector in India consciously built precautionary approaches to mitigate the ill effects of high fiscal deficits and large government borrowing programs. These measures were not exactly countercyclical but were in some ways macroprudential.

Although globally agreed-on standards of financial regulation would ensure coordination among national regulations as needed in a globalized world of finance, should there be emphasis on allowing for diversity in financial regulation among different countries? In the decade before the crisis of 2008, a globally binding model of best practices would have been the model practiced in London or New York. If that model had been adopted universally, China, India, and much of Asia in general would not have been leading the recovery. No one has a monopoly on universal wisdom on financial regulation. So how do we ensure diversity in financial regulation among countries in the future?

Whose Fault? Markets or the Government?

We formerly assumed that the failures of markets can be made up by the strengths of regulation, but the crisis has shown that market failures and regulatory failures reinforce each other. In the interactions between the market and government, governments can make up for market failures, they can interact with their strengths to synergize for the overall benefit, or they can reinforce each other's failures. The appropriate question may be how can we ensure that markets and regulations interface with each other to maximize social benefits and not collude or allow one to be captured or dominated by the other. Institutions like Fannie Mae and Freddie Mac in the United States were instruments of public policy, but they conducted their business no differently from their private-sector counterparts in terms of lobbying and tinkering with accounting standards. At the same time, public-sector banks in some other countries have been prudent and risk averse.

What accounts for differences in the economic behavior of instruments of public policy in different countries? Should public governance be different from the private sector in regard to values, checks and balances, incentives, and security of employment? Should those factors influence the relative roles of government and the market?

The Social Value of the Financial Sector?

The social value of the financial sector can be assessed in terms of its direct relevance (as a service to the average person in providing financial services) and its indirect relevance (through its resource mobilization and allocation, including managing risks and rewards).

The provision of financial services should be treated as public utility services and subject to regulation accordingly. A distinction in actual operations between the provision of financial services and intermediation is difficult, but it is necessary for a good design of public policy. The well-known Volcker rule attempts this.

Broadly, financial services may be defined as those that a common person would want from the financial sector and more generally are of direct social value. For example, people need the safe custody of cash and access to their cash when needed (the withdrawal of cash from automatic teller machines ensures equity in the quality of service). Second, citizens need one extremely safe instrument in which their savings can be kept for a rainy day. Third, the payment system should enable transfers of money between people in different locations with minimum inconvenience as well as cost. Fourth, resources need to be provided to smooth consumption when incomes are uneven over a period while the bulk of consumption is more stable (this requires access to credit facilities, but finance for the common person is often equated with personal credit to them). Finally, people participate in financial transactions as incidental to their normal lives, and the default option indicated by public policy should take account of these needs and not leave it to financial markets and regimes of contracts (between the financial intermediary and the everyday consumer) that are often among unequals. Have these social demands on the financial sector been assessed in regard to quality, coverage, or cost? Postcrisis, there are references to financial inclusion, but are there global standards or benchmarks for the purpose?

The social value of the financial sector is brought about indirectly in terms of the productive use of capital. Savers and investors have different risk and reward appetites and time horizons. It might be useful to explore empirical evidence in regard to having the financial sector enhance its role in mobilizing savings and allocating resources efficiently. Cross-country experiences seem to indicate that savings have been low in some of the countries where the financial sector is highly developed. Savings have been moderate or high in some countries where the banking system rather than the nonbanking system in the financial sector is dominant. What is the empirical evidence on the link between the level of saving, the efficient use of savings, and the level of development or nature of the financial sector?

In terms of cross-country flows, the empirical evidence shows that financial-sector development brought about a flow of resources to finance more consumption rather than savings in the developed financial sector. In most countries where the financial sector was highly developed, inequalities seem to have increased. What is the empirical cross-country evidence on developments in the financial sector and their implications for growth as well as equity? It appears that an optimal level and an optimal quality of financial-sector intermediation and sophistication seem to enable growth with stability but anything above these levels has not added fundamentally to society. In other words, are there an optimal level and complexity of the financial sector that optimize its social value?

How Active Should Regulation and Supervision Be?

If there are an optimal level and an optimal complexity of financial markets, which may be dynamic, then there may be a need to rebalance the regulatory regimes, with increasing regulation in some cases and decreasing regulation in others. In some countries, especially emerging-market economies, some deregulation of the financial sector may be needed to enable it to facilitate growth, but the extent of deregulation needs to take account of global experiences and local circumstances.

It is often argued that one reason for the crisis is that regulatory skills were not able to cope with market innovations. In the case of innovations, where should the benefit of the doubt rest—with the market or the regulator? For example, the safety of a drug has to be proved by the producer before it can be marketed, and for most other commodities, producers must pay a penalty if the product sold proves to be toxic. Where does a financial innovation lie within these two categories? One approach, adopted by the Reserve Bank of India (RBI), is that if the innovation's benefits do not convince the regulator of its safety, then it will not be permitted or permitted only with conditions (such as placing the burden of ensuring the proper criteria of the customer on the seller of the financial product).

After the crisis, several considerations appear to warrant a greater role for discretion than for rules. Countercyclical policies would involve assessment of structural and cyclical components. Such an assessment has subjective elements, and differentiation between the two is complex in emerging-market economies. The identification of systemically important institutions may warrant judgment. A financial intermediary that is not big may be a dominant player in a particular critical segment of financial market and thereby turn out to be systemically important. The issue in regulation and supervision is often one of effectiveness and not mere intensity. Effectiveness can be enhanced by a combination of early warning signals, preventive corrective actions, a graded escalating scale of effective penalties, and a wide range of instruments, to be applied with discretion. The actions of the regulator against the regulated cannot be based only on the transgression by an intermediary in individual instances or on technical compliance with a specific regulation. The regulator also must have an overall comfort with the conduct of business by a financial intermediary, consistent with the spirit of regulations. How extensive and how intensive should regulation be in normal circumstances, and how much additional discretion should be provided for meeting extraordinary circumstances?

Finally, the traditional debate between rules versus discretion in regulation may have to be restated. The new questions may be, how flexible should rules be, and what constraints should be imposed on discretion?

How to Design Financial Institutions?

Some financial institutions—say, in the United States and the United Kingdom—have been said to be too big to fail. At the same time, however, there can be financial institutions that are too big to save (examples can be found in Iceland). Other institutions that are important for a sector of the real economy or a segment of the financial markets may be not too big but too important or too critical to fail. There may also be financial institutions that are too powerful to regulate, owing to compulsions of domestic political economy or diplomatic considerations. When there are a few globally systemically important financial intermediaries that operate out of and with the strong governmental support of globally significant countries, they become too powerful to regulate. The situation is worse when the infrastructure, such as a few rating agencies and business news agencies, are also too important to fail. Can we influence the conduct of business by such entities by focusing regulations on standards of ownership and governance in relevant institutions? Will recognizing systemically important institutions and imposing higher capital requirements reduce or enhance the appetites of too powerful institutions for excessive risk? Should such institutions be stopped from emerging or existing?

How to Mitigate the Effects of Crisis?

Moral-hazard considerations compel large elements of constructive ambiguity in any strategy to mitigate the effects of crisis. It is possible to differentiate between a bailout of institutions and a bailout of their management and shareholders. Should we differentiate between the institutions whose continuity is critical to mitigating the effects of crisis and the managers and shareholders of these institutions that should be held responsible for the crisis? The power to dismiss executives, supersede the board of directors to replace management, and mandate the sale of shareholdings could be part of the package of unconventional measures that can mitigate the effects of crisis with minimum danger of moral hazard. In one case in India, a bank approached the Reserve Bank of India for liquidity support with full collateral, but liquidity was suspected of being denied to the bank by market participants owing to its questionable investments. The RBI made support conditional on the departure of the chief executive.

How Limited Is Our Understanding?

The cross-border activities of financial institutions are a big black box. The cross-border exposures have been a major source of collapse of many financial intermediaries in the crisis. In fact, much of the U.S. Federal Reserve's bailout packages helped resolve cross-border issues. Many financial institutions outside the United States faced a crisis because of overseas wholesale funding or lending. The nature of the regulation of many cross-border activities of financial intermediaries is unclear. Is it possible that the cross-border activities of financial institutions directly or indirectly contribute to undermining public policy in regard to regulations, taxes, and occasionally legality? How does volatility affect capital flows that are carried out by the cross-border activities of the financial sector on the real sector?

As it evolves, when does a financial sector stop playing the role of enabling the growth of the real economy and start injecting negative impulses into the real economy? When does the financial sector create wealth or value, and when does it divert wealth to itself from others? Further, should the real economy keep adjusting to the financial economy even when the latter is volatile for a prolonged period or deviates significantly owing to extraneous considerations? What are the differences between financial markets and nonfinancial markets? How do the two interact to enable enhancement of social value, create wealth, or divert wealth from many to a few? What kind of interaction occurs between banking and nonbanking sectors and between real and financial transactions in the financial sector?

Conflict-of-interest rules in the financial sector are often applied similarly in the public sector or regulator and in the private sector. There are advantages of coordination and also threats of conflicts of interests when there is an expanded mandate for regulators. Recent experience with crisis has shown that in public institutions, the benefits of coordination can prevail over the risks of conflicts of interest. In private institutions, despite the firewalls that were promised, the ill effects of conflicts of interests have prevailed. Should we change our regulatory structures relating to the coordination of conflict-of-interest rules in the public sector as distinct from the profit-driven private sector?

10
Global Liquidity

Hyun Song Shin

Low interest rates maintained by advanced-economy central banks in the aftermath of the global financial crisis that began in 2007 have ignited a lively debate about capital flows to emerging economies. The argument is that such capital flows are driven by carry trades that seek to exploit the interest-rate differences between advanced and emerging economies and that such flows result in overheating and excessively permissive financial conditions in the recipient country, posing challenges for policymakers.

The U.S. dollar has special significance in this debate. As well as being the world's most important reserve currency and an invoicing currency for international trade, the dollar is also the currency that underpins the global banking system. It is the funding currency of choice for global banks. The United States hosts branches of around 160 foreign banks whose main function is to raise wholesale dollar funding in capital markets and then ship it to their head office. Foreign bank branches collectively raise over $1 trillion of funding, of which over $600 billion is channeled to headquarters.[1] Figure 10.1 shows the interoffice assets of foreign bank branches in the United States—the lending by branches to headquarters. Interoffice assets increased steeply in the last two decades, saw a sharp decline in 2008, and bounced back in 2009.

It is instructive to compare the role of the dollar with that of the Japanese yen as a funding currency for global banks. Figure 10.2 plots the interoffice assets of foreign banks in Japan. Fueled by the yen carry trade, yen funding grew rapidly before the crisis but has subsequently been unwound in the aftermath of the crisis. Yen interoffice assets are now at their lowest level since the mid-1990s. The persistent strength of the yen after the crisis may be due in part to this unwinding. In net terms, global

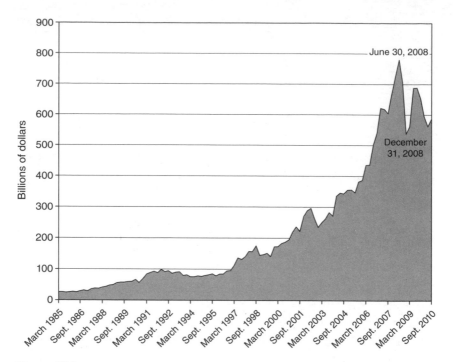

Figure 10.1
Interoffice assets of foreign bank branches in the United States. *Source:* Federal Reserve.

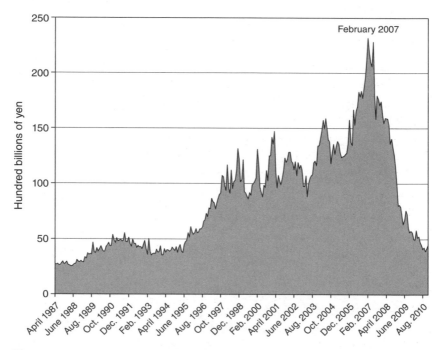

Figure 10.2
Interoffice assets of foreign bank branches in Japan. *Source:* Bank of Japan.

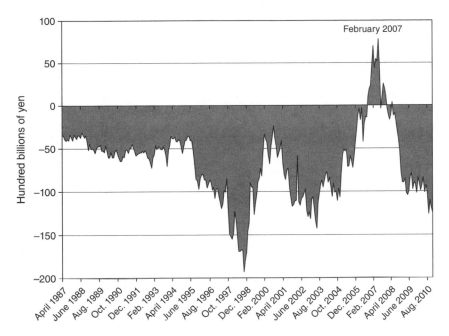

Figure 10.3
Net interoffice assets of foreign bank branches in Japan. *Source:* Bank of Japan.

banks have maintained negative interoffice accounts in yen, except for a brief period at the height of the boom before the global financial crisis, as can be seen in figure 10.3. In other words, the funds obtained from the head office for allocation in Japan have outweighed the yen shipped to headquarters.

However, what is remarkable about the U.S. dollar is that even in net terms, foreign banks have been channeling large amounts of dollar funding to the head office. Figure 10.4 shows the net interoffice assets of foreign banks in the United States. Net interoffice assets were negative in the 1980s and most of the 1990s, but in 1999, net interoffice assets surged into positive territory and increased steeply thereafter.[2]

We thus face an apparent paradox. Although the United States is the largest net debtor in the world, it is a substantial *net creditor* in the global banking system. In effect, the United States is borrowing long (through U.S. Treasury and other securities) but lending short through the banking sector. This is in contrast to countries such as Ireland and Spain that financed their current-account deficits through their respective banking

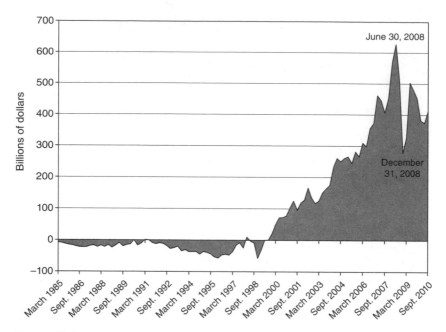

Figure 10.4
Net interoffice assets of foreign bank branches in the United States. *Source:* Federal Reserve.

sectors and that have subsequently paid the price through runs by wholesale creditors on their banks.

The large net positive interoffice accounts of foreign banks in the United States highlights the potential for cross-border spillovers in monetary policy. Dollar funding that is shipped abroad to headquarters will be deployed globally according to portfolio allocation decisions that seek out the most profitable use of such funds.

Some borrowed dollars will find their way back to the United States to finance purchases of mortgage-backed securities and other assets (remember UBS and its portfolio of subprime centralized debt obligations). But some will flow to Europe, Asia, and Latin America, where global banks are active local lenders. At the margin, the shadow value of bank funding will be equalized across regions through the portfolio decisions of the global banks so that global banks become carriers of dollar liquidity across borders. In this way, permissive U.S. liquidity conditions will be transmitted globally, and U.S. monetary policy becomes, in some respects, global monetary policy.

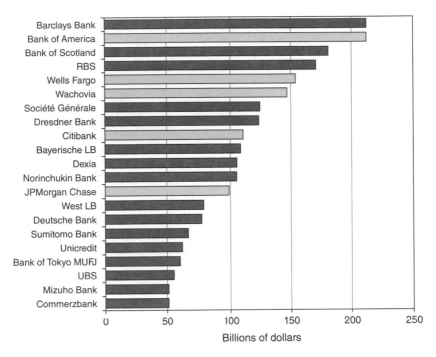

Figure 10.5
Cumulative borrowing under the Federal Reserve's term auction facility in twenty-one banks. *Source:* Federal Reserve.

A glimpse into the dollar's role as the funding currency of choice for global banks can be had in the identity of banks that took advantage of the emergency liquidity from the U.S. Federal Reserve during the crisis. Figure 10.5 shows the cumulative borrowing under the term auction facility (TAF) that allowed banks to receive term funding while avoiding the stigma of borrowing at the Fed's discount window. The light bars indicate U.S. banks, and the dark bars indicate non-U.S. banks. The cumulative total overstates the total support that was outstanding at any one time, given the repeated rollover of one month of term funding. But it is notable that the list is dominated by foreign banks, especially from Europe and Japan. Indeed, the largest borrower is Barclays, and three of the top four are U.K. banks.

After the foreign banks send wholesale dollar borrowings to their headquarters, the trail grows cold since we cannot peer into the internal global portfolio decisions of these banks. However, we can pick up the

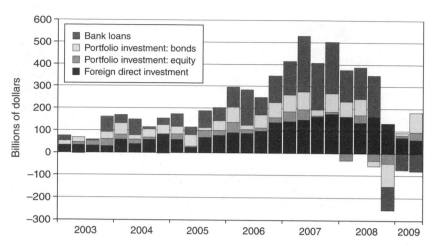

Figure 10.6
Components of U.S. capital flows to forty-one countries: loans, bonds, equity, foreign direct investment. *Source: Global Financial Stability Report* (April 2010), 123.

trail on the other side. Once the dollars are on loan to local borrowers in Europe, Asia, and Latin America, we can pick up the trail again by examining the banking-sector capital flows in the balance-of-payment accounts.

Figure 10.6 is a chart from the April 2010 issue of the International Monetary Fund's *Global Financial Stability Report*, showing total capital inflows into forty-one countries, including many emerging economies. The flows are disaggregated into the four main categories of capital flows—bank loans, bonds, equity, and foreign direct investment (FDI). We see that FDI flows are steady and portfolio equity flows are small in net terms. However, banking-sector flows display the signature procyclical pattern of surging during the boom, only to change sign abruptly and surge out with the deleveraging of the banking sector.

A more detailed picture emerges when we examine the noncore liabilities for the Korean banking sector, given in figure 10.7. The first peak comes immediately prior to the 1997 financial crisis. After a lull in the early 2000s, noncore liabilities again pick up speed and increase rapidly up to the 2008 financial crisis. Figure 10.8 normalizes noncore liabilities of the Korean banking sector as a fraction of M2 (bank deposits and close substitutes). We see the procyclicality and substantial variation,

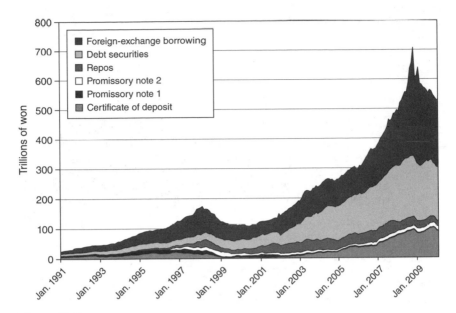

Figure 10.7
Noncore liabilities of the Korean banking sector. *Source:* Bank of Korea; Hyun Song Shin and Kwanho Shin, "Procyclicality and Monetary Aggregates," National Bureau of Economic Research Working Paper 16836 (2010), http://www.nber.org/papers/w16836.

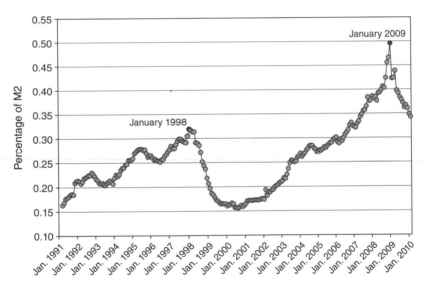

Figure 10.8
Noncore liabilities of the Korean banking sector as a proportion of M2. *Source:* Bank of Korea; Hyun Song Shin and Kwanho Shin, "Procyclicality and Monetary Aggregates," National Bureau of Economic Research Working Paper 16836 (2010), http://www.nber.org/papers/w16836.

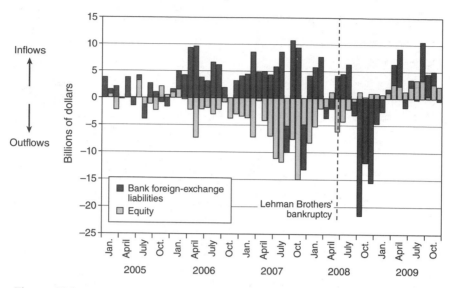

Figure 10.9
Net capital flows of the Korean equity and banking sector. *Source:* Bank of Korea; Hyun Song Shin and Kwanho Shin, "Procyclicality and Monetary Aggregates," National Bureau of Economic Research Working Paper 16836 (2010), http://www.nber.org/papers/w16836.

ranging from around 15 percent to a peak of 50 percent during the crisis of 2008.

The growth in foreign-currency liabilities and debt-security liabilities of Korean banks in the period between 2003 and 2007 (see figure 10.7) can be seen as the mirror image of the increase in net interoffice accounts of foreign banks in the United States (see figure 10.4). In effect, figure 10.4 reflects the liabilities side of global banks' balance sheets, and figure 10.7 reflects (a small part of) the asset side of global banks' balance sheets.

Figure 10.9 is a monthly chart of flows in the equity and the banking sectors in Korea. The equity sector actually saw net inflows during the crisis in the autumn of 2008, as selling by foreigners was more than matched by the repatriation flow of Korean investors who sold their holdings of foreign equity. However, the banking sector saw substantial outflows in the deleveraging episode following the bankruptcy of Lehman Brothers.

Letting the currency appreciate in response to capital inflows may mitigate the pressure from surging capital flows. However, when banking-sector flows form the bulk of the inflows and the leveraging and deleveraging cycle amplifies distortions to liquidity conditions, additional prudential measures may be necessary to lean against the buildup of vulnerabilities to sudden reversals and deleveraging.

Macroprudential policy that leans against the buildup of noncore banking-sector liabilities has some merit in this regard. Korea has announced that it will introduce a macroprudential levy in the form of a levy on the foreign-exchange-denominated liabilities of the banking sector, with a higher rate applying to short-term liabilities. The levy is intended to lean against excess liquidity and the buildup of vulnerabilities to the sudden reversals that are associated with deleveraging.

The levy can be expected to work as an automatic stabilizer since the base of the levy is larger during booms. The automatic stabilizer element is a virtue, given the political-economy impediments to relying on discretionary policy. Another advantage of the macroprudential levy is that it also leaves the core intermediation function largely untouched, operating primarily on the bubbly portion of the banking-sector liabilities.

Although the levy will have some effect on exchange rates, holding down the exchange rate should not be the primary objective of such a levy. By the same token, a debate that focuses exclusively on exchange rates and trade imbalances undervalues the financial stability role of macroprudential policy. Policymakers would do well to remember the main lesson from the global financial crisis—that the leveraging and deleveraging cycle of the banking sector is the driver of financial instability, for both advanced and emerging economies.

The IMF's Financial Stability Contribution (FSC) proposed a broad-based levy on the noncore liabilities of the banking system and could have been expected to exert some restraint on the leverage cycle of the global banks.[3] However, the IMF's FSC did not find sufficient support among the Group of Twenty governments and was shelved at the G20 Toronto summit in June 2010.

The failure of the G20 to adopt the FSC may reflect in part the framing of the debate in terms of raising revenue and "punishing" the banks. It may also reflect the dynamics of the complex multilateral process that the G20 represents. However, the imperative for well-designed macroprudential policies in a world with monetary policy spillovers increases the attractiveness of revisiting the merits of the FSC.

Notes

1. "Funding Patterns and Liquidity Management of Internationally Active Banks," Bank for International Settlements, Center for Global Financial Studies Paper 39 (May 2010), http://www.bis.org/publ/cgfs39.htm.

2. See http://www.federalreserve.gov/econresdata/releases/assetliab/current.htm.

3. See http://www.imf.org/external/np/g20/pdf/062710b.pdf.

11

Optimal Financial Intermediation: Why More Isn't Always Better

Adair Turner

How should the global economic crisis that began in 2008 affect our views about financial intermediation? This is a fundamental issue. We need to ask questions about the value of financial intermediation, about optimal levels of financial intermediation, and about reliance on free-market forces to select the optimal level and precise mix of financial intermediation.[1]

Over the last thirty years, financial intensity has grown remarkably, with increases in real-sector leverage but even more dramatic increases in financial-sector balance sheets as a percentage of gross domestic product, increases in trading volumes as a percentage of GDP, and the financial innovations of the derivatives market (figure 11.1). Before the crisis, the dominant conventional wisdom assumed and explicitly stated that this growth was beneficial because

- it would increase allocative efficiency since increased financial intensity completed more markets and because increased market liquidity ensured more efficient price discovery, and
- it would increase financial stability since risk would be dispersed more efficiently into the balance sheets of those best placed to manage it.

This conventional wisdom was strongly asserted, for instance, by the International Monetary Fund (2006).

The second half of the conventional wisdom proved wrong, and we need to understand why. There are two broad schools of thought:

- The first assumes that problems are essentially those of market imperfections, opacity, and perverse incentives. It seeks to identify the particular problems that prevented the system from reaching an efficient

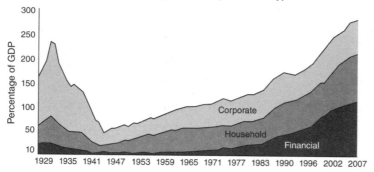

a. U.S. debt as a percentage of GDP by borrower type

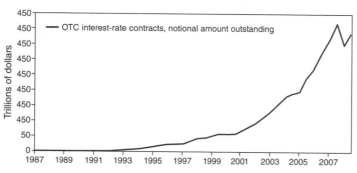

c. Growth of interest-rate derivatives values, 1987 to 2009

Figure 11.1
Measures of increasing financial intensity.

stable equilibrium and to put them right. This can be called the micro-structuralist school.

• The second believes that the drivers of instability are deeper than those amenable to increased transparency and the reform of incentives, and focuses on macroprudential oversight and policy response, including on a discretionary basis. This can be called the macro-Minsky school.

I comment on the relative merits of these two schools, express some preference for the latter, and support action to address incentives and structures as necessary but not sufficient.

The key problem that we are trying to solve is not the direct fiscal cost of the public rescue of otherwise failing banks. Although this is a key focus of popular outrage, the direct fiscal cost (as IMF figures show)

b. Global issuance of asset-backed securities

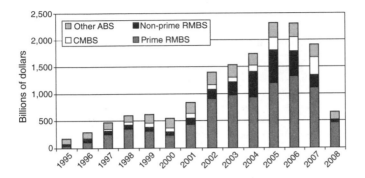

d. Foreign-exchange values and world GDP, 1977 to 2007

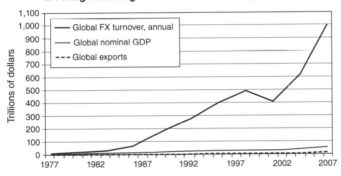

Figure 11.1
(cont.)

is the small change of the macroeconomic harm produced by bank failure (table 11.1). In some countries, it could turn out to be negative. Public authorities in total may make a profit from the combination of equity injections, debt guarantees, and central-bank operations.

Instead, the essential problem is the supply of credit, which first was provided in excessive quantity and at too low a price in a self-reinforcing cycle with asset prices (particularly real estate) and then was constricted, driving destructive and deflationary processes of overrapid deleveraging (figure 11.2). A key measure of the success of public-policy responses to the crisis is therefore whether they will reduce the amplitude of that cycle.

The structuralist school believes that if markets were made more efficient, and in particular if incentives were better aligned, then booms

Table 11.1
International Monetary Fund estimates of public-support costs in the 2008 to 2009 financial crisis

	Percentage of GDP			
	Pledged	Utilized	Recovery	Net direct cost
Advanced economies	6.2	3.5	0.8	2.8
Emerging economies	0.8	0.3	—	0.3

Source: International Monetary Fund, "A Fair and Substantial Contribution by the Financial Sector" (June 2010).

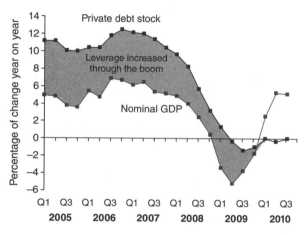

Figure 11.2
Growth in lending and nominal income: United Kingdom, 2005 to 2010.

and busts would naturally be constrained. The core policy is therefore to fix the too-big-to-fail problem. The assumption is that bankers and traders did excessively risky things—in both the banking and shadow banking systems—because they knew that they enjoyed the put option of limited liability.

We must certainly ensure the resolvability of too-big-to-fail banks—enabling us to impose losses on debt holders. This means smoothly turning debt claims into equity claims when necessary (figure 11.3). This is a necessary part of the reform process, and in circumstances where we face the future idiosyncratic failure of a large bank (the future equivalent of a Continental Illinois failure), it would also be a sufficient response.

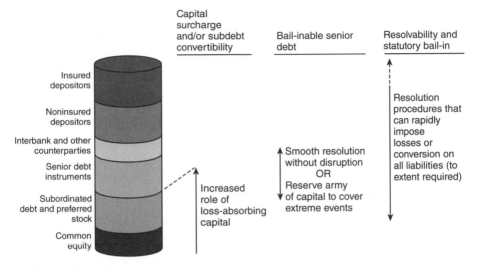

Figure 11.3
Mechanisms to increase loss absorption capacity and market discipline.

Table 11.2
Too big to fail: Conditions for success of debt-based solutions

Required to address the idiosyncratic failure of systemically important financial institutions:
Large enough percentage of balance sheet junior to depositors
Subject to write-down or conversion to equity in smooth process
Long enough in maturity to avoid precrisis runs
Additionally required to address systemic risks of multiple failures:
Held outside the banking system and by investors able to take losses without knock-on asset-first sale or debt-default consequences

But turning debt claims into equity claims is a sufficient response to future problems of systemic instability (and of the possible simultaneous, interconnected, and self-reinforcing failure of large banks or multiple small banks) only if we can assume three things—that bank debt instruments will be held by unleveraged, nonmaturity-transforming investors, that these investors are capable of taking losses without producing knock-on systemic effects, and that they can take losses without collectively acting in a way that generates self-reinforcing fire sales and a downward asset-price cycle (table 11.2).

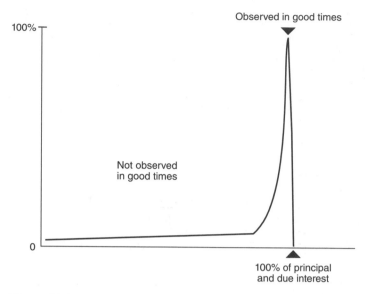

Figure 11.4
Frequency distribution of bank bond payouts.

These conditions would apply axiomatically if we can assume that investors always are foresightful and fully rational in their decisions—if they always consider the full range of future possible contingencies. But recent papers (such as Gennaioli, Shleifer, and Vishny 2010) challenge that assumption, arguing that many debt investors operate according to a model of local thinking in which during the good years they ignore the existence of the down tail of the distribution of possible results, essentially assuming that objectively risky instruments are close to risk free (figure 11.4).

As a result, the financial system—particularly if it is intense, complex, and innovative—is capable of generating an excessive quantity of debt instruments and a quantity of apparently risk-free instruments greater than can be objectively risk free, given the fundamental risk and indeed Knightian uncertainty inherently present in the real economy. When initial problems emerge, investors and depositors bring the down tail of the distribution into their consciousness and decision-making processes, generating self-reinforcing downward cycles of confidence, liquidity, asset prices, and credit supply.

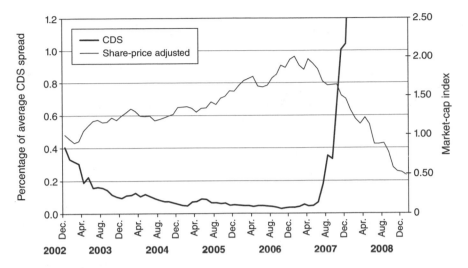

Figure 11.5
Financial firms' credit default swaps (CDSs) and share prices. *Source:* Moody's KMV; Financial Services Authority calculations.

Shleifer's analysis fits well with what actually occurred in 2000 to 2007 to 2009 (figure 11.5). For instance, the credit default swap spreads of major banks fell to historically low levels in June 2007, immediately ahead of the crisis; the discovered market price first provided us with no useful forewarning of impending problems before the crisis but then swung to excessive overreaction.

Shleifer's analysis means that both incentives and myopia can be problems. If that is the case, then fixing incentives is highly desirable but insufficient to ensure stability. The implication of this in relation to the too-big-to-fail debate is that we should strongly prefer solutions that increase the equity ratios of large systemically important financial institutions (SIFIs) because only with equity instruments can we be reasonably certain that the instruments will be held by investors that are able to take losses without knock-on systemic consequences. More generally, this illustrates that the core issues of financial stability are (1) the balance within the economy between debt and equity contracts and (2) the aggregate maturity transformation that the financial system is in total performing.

Table 11.3
Rigidities and vulnerabilities of debt contracts

• Bankruptcy costs: nonsmooth adjustment
• Fire-sale costs
• Need for continual rollover
• Multiple equilibria, depending on interest rate
• Credit and asset-price cycles

An economy has equity and debt contracts. Debt contracts, like fixed-wage contracts, respond to people's desire for apparent certainty in income flow. Not all contracts express equity partner shares in the underlying value added that economic projects produce (Einaudi 2006). But debt instruments introduce into the economy important potential rigidities, irreversibilities, and procyclical tendencies (table 11.3). These arise from a combination of the institutions of bankruptcy, the possibility of fire sales, the need for debt to be rolled over continually, the existence of multiple equilibria depending on an endogenously determined credit-risk spread, and self-reinforcing credit and asset-price cycles.

Together these mean that cycles of irrational exuberance in debt markets are inherently more dangerous than equivalent cycles in equity markets. The Internet equity-price boom and bust of 1995 to 2000 to 2002 produced large individual wealth gains and losses but little macroeconomic harm. Debt cycles, as both IMF analysis and Reinhart and Rogoff (2009) have shown, produce far greater harm. Therefore, the total extent of leverage in the real economy and in the financial system is an important macrovariable.

But also important is the aggregate degree of maturity transformation—the extent to which the financial system in total, whether through bank balance sheets or via liquid markets, enables the nonfinancial sector to hold financial assets of shorter-term maturity than liabilities. This vital and socially value-creative transformation function produces a yield structure of interest rates more favorable to long-term investment than would otherwise exist. But it is also inherently risky.

Measuring aggregate financial system maturity transformation is therefore vital, but its difficulty increases as the financial intermediation system becomes more complex, interconnected, and multistage. For several decades before the crisis, aggregate maturity transformation increased. Households, for instance, accumulated far more long-term liabilities (mortgages), but the household and corporate assets that funded these were predominantly short term—a development that, fatally, we failed to understand.

In the future, we need to monitor aggregate leverage and aggregate maturity transformation, and we cannot assume that the financial system, left to itself (even with better incentives in place), will select the optimal levels of leverage and maturity transformation. We need policy instruments that are designed to influence those key macro stability parameters.

Levels are important, with high levels of either leverage or maturity transformation creating vulnerability, but changes in levels (that is, cycles) are also important. It is unclear whether any set of constant rules can be relied on to limit occasional excess cyclicality. Also necessary, therefore, is a degree of countercyclical discretion for leaning against credit and asset-price cycles.

So I am arguing that the second half of the precrisis conventional wisdom—that increased financial intensity, complexity, and innovation would ensure stability—was wrong. Empirically, it was proved so, and the theoretical reasons why it was wrong can be identified.

But where does this leave the first question, about whether increased financial intensity and complexity deliver allocative efficiency benefits? I cannot address this important question in this chapter, but I would like to finish with two points.

First, we cannot assume axiomatically that increasing financial intensity produces valuable allocative efficiency benefits. A wealth of theory suggests that financial intensity can be rent extracting rather than value creative and that any beneficial effect of increasing financial intensity in terms of allocative efficiency must be subject to declining marginal returns.

Second, the answer to this question has implications for financial stability policy. Many of the measures that could be taken to increase stability—such as higher capital requirements against trading activities or against intrafinancial system claims—might reduce the scale of trading activity and the liquidity of some markets. If these activities and related liquidity are value creative (at the social level), then we may need to make a tradeoff between stability and allocative efficiency. If they are zero sum or rent extracting, then there is no such tradeoff. The less certain we are that increased financial activity delivers improved allocative efficiency, the more radical we can be in the pursuit of stability-oriented reforms.

Note

1. These comments present a summary of conclusions that were set out in more detail in a lecture that was delivered at Clare College, Cambridge: "Reforming Finance: Are We Being Radical Enough?," available at www.fsa.gov.uk/Pages/Library/Communication/Speeches/index.shtml.

References

Einaudi, Luigi. 2006. *Debts: Selected Economic Essays.* Basingstoke, UK: Palgrave Macmillan. Originally published as *Debiti* (Rome: La Reforma Societe, January 1934).

Gennaioli, Nicola, Andrei Shleifer, and Robert Vishny. 2010. *Neglected Risks, Financial Innovation, and Financial Fragility.* FEEM Working Paper No. 111.2010. Rome: Fondazione Eni Enrico Mattei, September.

International Monetary Fund. 2006. *Global Financial Stability Report: Market Developments and Issues* (April). http://www.imf.org/external/pubs/ft/GFSR/2006/01/index.htm.

Reinhart, Carmen M., and Kenneth S. Rogoff. 2009. *This Time Is Different: Eight Centuries of Financial Folly.* Princeton, NJ: Princeton University Press.

12

Process, Responsibility, and Myron's Law

Paul Romer

In the wake of the financial crisis, any rethinking of macroeconomics has to include an examination of the rules that govern the financial system. This examination needs to take a broad view that considers the ongoing dynamics of those rules. It will not be enough to come up with a new set of specific rules that seem to work for the moment. We need a system in which the specific rules in force at any point in time evolve to keep up with a rapidly changing world.

A diverse set of examples suggests that there are workable alternatives to the legalistic, process-oriented approach that characterizes the current financial regulatory system in the United States. These alternatives give individuals responsibility for making decisions and hold them accountable. In this sense, the choice is not really between legalistic and principle-based regulation. Instead, it is between process and responsibility.

The Dynamics of Rules

The driving force of economic life is the nonrivalry of ideas. *Nonrivalry* means that each idea has a value proportional to the number of people who use it. Nonrivalry creates a force that pushes for increases in the scale of interaction. We see this force in globalization, which relies on flows of goods to carry embedded ideas to ever more people. We see it in digital communication, which allows the direct sharing of ideas among ever more people. We see it in urbanization, which allows us to share ideas in face-to-face exchanges with ever more people.

A new slant on an old saying expresses the updated essence of nonrivalry of a technological idea: give someone a fish, and you feed them for a day; teach someone to fish, and you destroy another aquatic ecosystem. This update reflects what has happened throughout most of human history and warns that we need more than new ideas about technology to achieve true progress.

We need to broaden our list of ideas to include the rules that govern how humans interact in social groups (rules like those that limit the total catch in a fishery). *Rules* in this sense mean any regularities of human interaction, regardless of how they are established and enforced. Finding good rules is not a one-time event. As academics, policymakers, and students of the world, we need to think about the dynamics of both technologies and rules.

To achieve efficient outcomes, our rules need to evolve as new technologies arrive. They must also evolve in response to the increases in scale that nonrivalry induces. Finally, and perhaps most important, they also need to evolve in response to the opportunistic actions of individuals who try to undermine them. Myron Scholes once captured this last effect in a statement he made in a seminar, a statement that deserves to be immortalized as Myron's law:

Asymptotically, any finite tax code collects zero revenue.

His point was that if there is a fixed set of rules in something like a tax code, clever opportunists will steadily undermine their effectiveness. They will do this, for example, by changing the names of familiar objects to shift them between different legal categories or by winning judicial rulings that narrow the applicability of the existing rules.

In sum, rules have to evolve in response to three distinct factors—new technologies, increases in the scale of social interaction, and opportunistic attempts at evasion. Any social group has higher-level rules—*metarules*—that determine how specific rules evolve. The metarules that govern the tax code, for example, allow for changes through legislation passed by Congress, regulations written by the Internal Revenue Service, and rulings handed down by courts. In some domains, the three forces that call for more rapid change in the rules may operate with greater force. In those domains, we presumably want to rely on different metarules.

Why Rules Lag Behind

As the number of people who use the Internet has increased, the rules that govern behavior have lagged far behind actual practice. This case offers helpful illustrations about the general problem that we face ensuring that rules keep up.

New technologies are part of the problem. Digital communication has created many new possibilities for criminal activity that crosses national borders. Our systems of criminal investigation and prosecution, which are based on geographical notions of jurisdiction, are ill-suited to this new world.

Scale also has an independent effect. Email is based on a set of rules that worked well when dozens of academics were communicating with each other. These informal rules were based on norms and reputation, so the Internet protocol and associated protocols for managing email failed to include even the most basic protections. Now that the Internet has scaled from dozens of people to billions, different rules are needed. For example, there is no built-in way for the recipient of an email to be sure about the identity of the sender. In a "spear-phishing" attack, an email is carefully tailored to resemble the authentic emails that the recipient normally receives. Because none of the usual warning signs are present (there are no offers of millions of dollars stranded in a stranger's bank account), the recipient is more likely to open an attachment with malicious code. Even RSA, a company whose business revolves around computer security, was compromised through this kind of attack.

Engineers at the Internet Engineering Task Force, a loosely defined voluntary organization with little formal authority, are the rule setters for the Internet. In 1992, they began to work on improving security protocols. They devised a patch called IPsec that reverse-engineered some basic security measures into the existing protocol. They also developed an update to the basic Internet protocol, known as IPv6, that has built-in support for IPsec. The basic specifications for these protocols were completed in 1998. Unfortunately, larger scale not only creates the need for better security but also makes it much harder to implement a change in the rules. The adoption of both sets of protocols has been held back by coordination problems among large numbers of users and vendors.

Even if these protocols are widely adopted, new attacks will still emerge. Bigger scale means that traditional mechanisms like reputation no longer operate and that more people are working to undermine and subvert all the existing security measures. Because a new vulnerability is a nonrival good that can be shared among predators, an increase in scale can increase the rate at which predators circumvent any given security system.

Financial Markets

Rules in financial markets need to evolve for all of the reasons identified above. Technology is creating entirely new opportunities—for example, in high-frequency electronic trading systems. The scale of financial markets continues to grow, and private actors in these markets will surely seek clever ways to evade the intent of existing rules. The gains from opportunism in these markets are so large that the total amount of human effort directed at evading the rules will presumably be at least as large as that devoted to a low-return activity like cybercrime.

Electronic transactions were supposed to offer liquid markets and unified prices that can be accessed by everyone, but they have not lived up to this promise because they have also created new opportunities for manipulation. For example, some firms now submit and withdraw very large numbers of electronic quotes within milliseconds in a practice known as *quote stuffing*. It is not clear what the intent of these traders is, but it is clear that any electronic trading system will have capacity constraints in computation and communication. Any system will therefore be subject to congestion. In the May 2010 stock market flash crash, congestion added to the anomalous behavior that firms were observing, and this apparently encouraged many high-frequency traders to stop trading, at least temporarily. This seems to have contributed to the temporary sharp fall in prices.

Quote stuffing could be one of many different strategies that traders use to influence local congestion and delays in the flow of information through the trading system. These, in turn, could affect liquidity, as they did during the flash crash. As a result, transactions could take place at prices that depart substantially from those that prevailed just before or just after they occurred.

After an extensive analysis, the Securities and Exchange Commission (SEC) reported that quote stuffing was not the source of the cascade of transactions that overwhelmed the systems during the flash crash. The SEC is still equivocating about whether this particular practice is harmful and, more generally, about systemic problems that high-frequency traders may be causing. Even if it had tried to address the specific practice of quote stuffing, the type of rule that had first been mooted—forcing traders to wait 50 milliseconds before withdrawing a quote that they had just submitted—would probably have been too narrow to limit the many other strategies that could be used to generate congestion or influence liquidity.

It seems implausible that the kind of behavior that occurred in the flash crash is an inevitable consequence of electronic trading. (But if it is, it seems implausible that the switch to electronic trading has brought net welfare benefits for the economy as a whole.) One year later, it also seems implausible that any of the changes implemented so far has fully addressed the underlying issue. Individual stocks continue to suffer from instances where trades take place at prices that are dramatically different from those that are prevailing seconds before or seconds later.

After the flash crash, trades were canceled if they took place at prices that differed from a reference price by more than a discretionary threshold, set in that particular case as a 60 percent deviation. Under new rules that try to be more explicit, transactions for some individual stocks will be allowed to stand if they take place at prices within 10 percent of the a reference price. In a multistock event, where many prices move together, the band of acceptability widens to 30 percent. Some have criticized these new rules because they still allow some discretion in setting the reference price. Others have expressed concern about the potential for manipulation that could intentionally trigger the looser rules that apply in a multistock event.

As the discussion below about rule making at the Occupational Safety and Health Administration (OSHA) shows, even in a simple setting it is difficult to develop rules in a timely fashion that meet legal standards for clarity and do so following procedures that meet legal standards for due process. The Security and Exchange Commission's attempts to clarify the rules for breaking trades suggest that it is much harder to live up to these standards in a complicated and dynamic context. The SEC seems to have settled for a rule-setting process that leaves ample room for opportunism for extended periods of time. Perhaps some other, less legalistic approach deserves consideration.

Process versus Responsibility in Other Domains

One way to think about how the metarules that govern financial regulation might be adjusted so that the system can respond more quickly is to examine a broad range of social domains and observe the outcomes under alternative metarules. Here are four influential organizations in the United States that set rules and a specific goal that each organization's rules try to promote:

- Federal Aviation Administration (FAA): flight safety
- Federal Reserve: stable economic activity
- U.S. Army: combat readiness
- Occupational Safety and Health Administration (OSHA): worker safety

The Federal Aviation Administration works in a domain with the potential for rapid technological evolution. It has responsibility for passenger airplanes, which are among the most complex products ever developed. It approaches its task of ensuring flight safety with rules that specify required outcomes but that are not overly precise about the methods by which these outcomes are to be achieved. This is one way to interpret what principle-based regulation should look like. In practice, this means that some person must have responsibility for interpreting how any specific act, in a specific situation, either promotes or detracts from the goal that is implicit in the principle. That is, someone has to take responsibility for making a decision.

The general requirement that the FAA places on a new plane is that the manufacturer demonstrate to the satisfaction of its examiners that the new airplane is airworthy. The examiners use their judgment to decide what this means for a new type of plane. Within the FAA, the examiners are held responsible for their decisions. This changes the burden of proof from the regulators of a new technology to the advocates of the technology and gives FAA examiners a large measure of flexibility.

This approach stands in sharp contrast to one based on process. There is no codified process that a manufacturer can follow and be guaranteed that a new plane will be declared airworthy. Nor is there a codified process that the FAA examiners can follow in making a determination about airworthiness. There is no way for them to hide behind a defense that they "checked all the boxes" in the required process.

One obvious requirement for a plane to be airworthy is that the airframe be sufficiently strong. There are no detailed regulations that specify the precise steps that a manufacturer must use to make a plane strong or show that it is strong. For example, there are no regulations about the size or composition of the rivets that hold the skin on the airframe, nor should there be. On an airplane like the Boeing 787, which is made of composite materials, there are no rivets. Instead, as part of the general process of establishing airworthiness, the employees of the FAA have technical expertise in areas like materials science and testing procedures and are responsible for making a judgment about how to test a particular design and determine whether it is sufficiently strong.

Moreover, because new information about an airframe can emerge for decades after it enters into service, the granting of a certificate of airworthiness is always provisional. Operators of aircraft are required to report evidence that emerges over time that might be relevant to airworthiness. At any time, the FAA can withdraw a plane's airworthiness certificate or mandate changes that must be made to an aircraft for it to continue to be airworthy. No judicial proceeding is required. There is no appeal process for an owner that unexpectedly receives an airworthiness directive that mandates an expensive modification. There is no way to get a judge to issue an injunction that would let the plane keep flying because the FAA has not satisfied some procedural requirement.

It is also clear that the rate of innovation in technologies is a choice variable, along with the rate of innovation in the rules. If social returns are maximized when technologies and rules stay roughly in sync, good metarules might require that those who develop new technologies also have to develop the complementary rules before the new technologies can be implemented. A larger plane such as the Airbus 380 will generate more air turbulence in its wake. This means that the FAA has to implement new rules about the spacing between planes that follow each other on a flight path. The FAA will not let a plane like the Airbus 380 fly until the manufacturer has demonstrated the size of its wake and the FAA has had time to put in place new systemwide rules about separation. This is the polar opposite of the approach that the SEC takes with regard to the introduction of major changes in the architecture of the electronic trading system.

The FAA implements a system based on individual responsibility by organizing itself as a hierarchy. People at a higher level can promote and sanction people at lower levels based on how well they do their jobs. At the top of the hierarchy, the secretary of transportation and the administrator of the FAA are appointed by the president and confirmed by Congress, both of which are held accountable by the electorate.

The Federal Reserve, like every other central bank, is also organized as a hierarchy. Its leaders are held accountable by democratically elected officials who specify a mandate. In their day-to-day decisions, the employees at lower levels in the hierarchy have a lot of freedom to take actions that will achieve the organization's mandate. They are rewarded or punished based on the judgment of those one level higher in the hierarchy. There is little scope for the legislature to micromanage decisions, and there is no judicial review of the process by which decisions are made. As was seen in the financial crisis of 2009, this kind of system allowed for a much quicker response than the parallel mechanism involving legislation passed by Congress. The Fed's response to the failure of Long Term Capital Management also showed that it could manage what amounted to a bankruptcy reorganization far more quickly than a court could.

Like the Fed and the FAA, the U.S. Army is run as a hierarchy, with accountability at the top to elected officials. After a period during the 1970s when racial tensions in the army were seriously undermining its effectiveness, the leaders of the army decided that better race relations were essential for it to meet its basic goal of combat readiness. In less than two decades, they remade the organization. Writing in 1996, the sociologists Charles Moskos and John Butler observed that among large organizations in the United States, the army was "unmatched in its level of racial integration" and "unmatched in its broad record of black achievement" (2). To illustrate how different the army was from more familiar institutions such as the universities where they worked, Moskos and Butler (1996, 3) tell this story:

Consciousness of race in a nonracist organization is one of the defining qualities of Army life. The success of race relations and black achievement in the Army revolves around this paradox. A story several black soldiers told us at Fort Hood,

Texas, may help illustrate this point. It seems that one table in the dining facility had become, in an exception to the rule, monopolized by black soldiers. In time, a white sergeant came over and told the blacks to sit at other tables with whites. The black soldiers resented the sergeant's rebuke. When queried, the black soldiers were quite firm that a white soldier could have joined the table had one wished to. Why, the black soldiers wondered, should they have to take the initiative in integrating the dining tables?

The story has another remarkable point—that a white sergeant should take it on himself to approach a table of blacks with that kind of instruction. The white sergeant's intention, however naive or misdirected, was to end a situation of racial self-segregation. Suppose that a white professor asked black students at an all-black table in a college dining hall to sit at other tables with whites. This question shows the contrast between race relations on college campuses and in the army.

The system in the army makes such individuals as the sergeant in this story responsible for the state of race relations in any unit they supervise. This system holds them responsible for both their decisions and accomplishments, through occasional ad hoc review of their decisions by superior officers and through more formal decisions about promotion to a higher rank. Any particular decision like that of the sergeant in the story could easily be second-guessed, but the system as a whole has clearly been effective at achieving both integration and good race relations. Both direct judicial intervention in the operation of public school systems and the combination of legislation and regulations that guide behavior on university campuses have been far less successful.

The approaches to safety at the FAA, to macroeconomic stabilization at the Fed, and to race relations in the army all stand in sharp contrast to the legalistic, process-centered approach to safety followed by OSHA. To improve safety on construction sites, which have a bad safety record, OSHA follows a detailed process that leads to the publication of specific regulations such as these:

1926. 1052(c)(3)
The height of stair rails shall be as follows:
1926. 1052(c)(3)(i)
Stair rails installed after March 15, 1991, shall be not less than 36 inches (91.5 cm) from the upper surface of the stair rail system to the surface of the tread, in line with the face of the riser at the forward edge of the tread.
1926. 1052(c)(3)(ii)
Stairrails installed before March 15, 1991, shall be not less than 30 inches (76 cm) nor more than 34 inches (86 cm) from the upper surface of the stair rail

system to the surface of the tread, in line with the face of the riser at the forward edge of the tread.

These regulations are enforced by OSHA inspectors, who can issue citations that lead to fines and that can then be challenged in court. The regulations are supplemented by guidance about enforcement. For example, in the early 1990s, someone also added a note in the *Construction Standard Alleged Violations Elements (SAVE) Manual* that guided OSHA inspectors on how to apply these regulations on stair rails:

NOTE: Although 29 CFR 1926.1052(c)(3)(ii) sets height limits of 30"–34" for stairways installed before March 15, 1991, no citation should be issued for such rails if they are 36" maximum with reference to 29 CFR 1926.1052(c)(3)(i).

This change in enforcement patterns avoids the awkward situation in which a 35-inch-high rail could be cited either for being too low or for being too high, depending on when it was installed, although it still leaves a puzzle about why a 38-inch-high rail might still be cited if it had been installed too early.

It is tempting to ridicule regulations like these, but it is more informative to adopt the default assumption that the people who wrote them are as smart and dedicated as the people who work at the FAA. From this, it follows that differences in what the two types of government employees actually do must be traced back to structural differences in the metarules that specify how their rules are established and enforced. The employees at the FAA have responsibility for flight safety. They do not have to adhere to our usual notions of legalistic process and are not subject to judicial review. In contrast, employees of OSHA have to follow a precise process specified by law to establish or enforce a regulation. The judicial checks built into the process mean that employees at OSHA do not have any real responsibility for worker safety. All they can do is follow the process.

One possible interpretation of the regulations about stair rails is that the regulations once specified a maximum height of 34 inches and that new evidence emerged showing that a higher rail would be safer. As they considered new rules they could propose, the regulation writers faced the question of what rules to apply to stairways that had been installed in the past. Rather than make an ex post change to the regulations for existing stairs, they may have chosen instead to stick to the principle that the regulations that were in force when a stairway was installed would continue to apply to that stairway but to suspend enforcement for some violations.

The caution about ex post changes in the regulations may derive in part from a concern about judicial review of the new rules. Or it could have come from a concern about judicial review of penalties that had already been assessed or violations under the old rules that would no longer be violations under the new rules. The change in enforcement at least made sure that no judge saw cases where 35-inch-high rails were sometimes cited for being too high and sometimes for being too low.

You can get some sense of how difficult it is to be precise in writing rules by digging into an area like this. From published inquiries that OSHA received, it seems that the decisions here were complicated by ambiguity about the rules for handrails, which a person uses as a grip and should therefore not be too high, and stair rails, which mark the top of a barrier designed to prevent falls and which therefore should not be too low. The top of a stair rail might be but need not be a handrail. It looks as though the rules morphed over time to distinguish more explicitly between the two types of rails.

It is striking that safety officers for construction firms who wrote to OSHA for clarifications about apparent discrepancies between different sections of the regulations waited four to six months to receive answers. (One wonders what happened at the construction sites during those many months.)

Even more striking is the fact that the rules cited here were first proposed in 1990 or 1991, but judging from a 2005 notice in the *Federal Register* calling once again for comments, they did not come into force until sometime after 2005. (The notice in 2005 makes a brief reference to other agency priorities that took precedence over the rules for stair rails.) This required the application of a further enforcement instruction that a stair rail that conforms to the proposed regulation for stairs built after 1991 but that violates the existing regulations (which were not changed for another fifteen years) would be treated as a de minimus violation and would not result in an enforcement action.

The principle-based approach to the regulation of air safety lacks all of the procedural and legal protections afforded by the process of OSHA, but in terms of the desired outcomes, the FAA approach seems to work better. Air travel is much safer than working on a construction site. The

Fed and the army also seem to have been much more effective in addressing complicated challenges. Despite the more extensive judicial protections afforded the construction firms under the OSHA process, firms find the process infuriating. Construction sites are still very dangerous places to work.

Conclusion

People from the United States take pride in a shared belief that theirs is "a nation of laws, not of individual men and women." Taken literally, this claim is nonsense. Any process that decides what kind of planes can carry passengers, what to do during a financial panic, how people of different races interact, or how a construction site is organized will have to rely on decisions by men and women.

Because of combinatorial explosion, the world presents us with a nearly infinite set of possible circumstances. No language with a finite vocabulary can categorize all these different circumstances. No process that writes rules in such a language can cover all these circumstances. Laws and regulations always require interpretation. Giving judges a role to play in making these interpretations or reviewing them does not take people out of the process.

We could have a system in which individual financial regulators have the same kind of responsibility and authority as the sergeant in the cafeteria. If they saw behavior that looked harmful to the system, they could unilaterally stop it. We could have a system like the one we use to certify passenger aircraft, in which the burden of demonstrating that an innovation does not threaten the safety of the entire trading system rests on those who propose the innovation. In such a system, the people that the innovators would have to persuade could be specialists who would have the same kind of responsibility and authority as FAA examiners. The opportunists in the financial sector would presumably prefer to stay with an approach that emphasizes process, but this leaves the other participants in the sector at a relative disadvantage. More seriously, it leaves those outside the sector unprotected, with no one who takes responsibility for limiting the harms that the sector can cause.

The right question to ask is not whether people are involved in enforcing a system of rules but rather which people are involved and which incentives they operate under. There may be some contexts where a legalistic approach like that followed by OHSA and the SEC has advantages, but we need to recognize that this approach is not the only alternative and that it has obvious disadvantages.

A careful weighing of the costs and benefits will involve many factors, but the factor that seems particularly important for the financial sector concerns time constants. As the OSHA example suggests, the legalistic process is inherently much slower than a process that gives individuals more responsibility. Moreover, clever opportunists can dramatically increase the delays and turn the legalistic approach into what Phillip Howard (2010) calls a "perpetual process machine."

Under this approach, rules for the financial sector will never keep up. The technology is evolving too quickly. The scale of the markets is enormous and continues to grow. There may be no other setting in which opportunism can be so lucrative. It is hard to understand why technologically sophisticated people devote any effort to committing cybercrime when the payoffs from opportunism in financial markets seem to be so much larger. If we persist with the assumption that a legalistic rule-setting process is the only conceivable one we could use to regulate financial markets, then the opportunists will thrive. We will settle into a fatalistic acceptance of systemic financial crises, flash crashes, and ever more exotic forms of opportunism.

"No one can predict how complicated software systems will behave" (except in airplanes). "You can't change behavior" (except in the army). "Financial systems are just too complicated to regulate" (except in countries like Canada, where instead of running a process, regulators take responsibility).

References

Howard, Philip K. 2010. "To Cut the Deficit, Get Rid of Surplus Laws." *Washington Post*, December 10.

Moskos, Charles C., and John Sibley Butler. 1996. *All That We Can Be: Black Leadership and Racial Integration the Army Way*. New York: Basic Books.

IV

Capital-Account Management

Questions: How Should the Crisis Affect Our Views of Capital-Account Management?

The economic crisis that began in 2008 revealed the tight links that financial globalization has created across countries. Large capital outflows at the height of the crisis created serious funding problems. Balance-sheet effects, affecting either ultimate borrowers or financial intermediaries, often led to perverse effects of depreciation.

The environment since the peak of the crisis shows the tensions coming instead from large capital inflows. Many emerging-market countries are considering—and some are implementing—capital controls. They often blame policies in advanced countries, from low interest rates to quantitative easing, for generating excessive and volatile capital flows.

How should countries deal with financial openness—specifically, capital flows? What combination of macropolicy and macroprudential responses should they use, and when should capital controls come into play? What should be the rules of the game?

Macroeconomic Response

What is the right macroeconomic response to high capital inflows? The basic principles laid down by the International Monetary Fund are that the country should use monetary and fiscal policy with three objectives in mind: let the exchange rate appreciate to the point where it is fairly valued, do not accumulate reserves beyond precautionary needs, and try to maintain output close to potential to maintain stable inflation.

Are these the right principles? And what do they mean in practice? Suppose a country had a correctly valued exchange rate before capital flows increased. What is the "correct" exchange rate given the increase in capital flows? Just like the exchange rate, the appropriate level of reserves depends on the flows themselves. So what is the appropriate level of reserves in this context?

The Macroprudential Response and the Role of Capital Controls

What is the right macroprudential response to high capital flows? Tentative principles might be that macroprudential tools—including balance-sheet restrictions, loan-to-value ratios, and foreign exposure limits—can be used to limit the adverse effects of high inflows on either macro or financial fragility. If these measures are still insufficient (for example, if capital flows are not intermediated and thus not easily subject to macroprudential tools), then (and only then) capital controls should be considered. Are these the right principles? Why should capital controls come last in the list? If ruling out discrimination against foreign residents justifies the ordering, then what should be done about macroprudential measures, such as foreign exposure limits, which often discriminate against nonresidents in practice and have a clear effect on capital flows?

Multilateral Rules of the Game?

More generally, what should be the rules of the game (if any) in terms of reserve accumulation and in terms of capital controls? Reserve accumulation beyond a reasonable precautionary saving level may or may not be in the interest of a country, but shouldn't that be left up to the country to decide? Or should it be banned on multilateral grounds? Should countries be left to choose whether to use capital controls? Or should there be multilateral rules as well, and if the answer is yes, can realistic rules be designed? Do the countries of origin also have some responsibility? Suppose, for example, that the main effect of the Federal Reserve's second round of quantitative easing is to encourage carry-trade-type flows. Should the Federal Reserve be restrained? If so, does the argument extend to monetary policy more generally?

13

Notes on Capital-Account Management

Ricardo Caballero

In this chapter, I look at two sets of capital-account issues—country-specific dilemmas in dealing with large capital inflows and global equilibrium issues.

Country-Specific Issues

What are the conditions under which a real appreciation caused by large inflows is a problem? There are many specific channels through which a problem can arise, but the generic concern is that somehow the medium- and long-run health of the economy will be compromised by a sustained appreciation. To justify policy intervention, these concerns must be about externalities, either pecuniary or technological. I focus on the former.

A pecuniary externality can arise when there is limited domestic financial development and the export sector is not able to ride a temporary capital inflow spike despite its positive net present value. Even if capital flows are permanent, following, for example, a major oil reserve discovery, the speed of the appreciation may be too much for the noncommodity export sector to fund the required retooling.

To understand the mechanism, think about a temporary capital inflow that expands domestic expenditure and hence appreciates the real exchange rate. There is a potential for a negative externality in this context, even if we completely disregard the welfare of export producers. Consider what happens when the temporary capital inflow goes away. If the export sector is financially damaged, then it will take a much larger real depreciation (and hence expenditure contraction) for it to absorb the labor force released from nontradables. If consumers collectively could internalize this effect, then they would contain the initial surge in expenditure to reduce the real appreciation and its damage on a financially constrained exports sector. In this context, economic policy is a substitute for the lack of coordinated foresight of domestic consumers.

A second branch of externality arises from a domestic financial system that has its own agency problems, which are exacerbated by cheap external funding. Here the main direct problem is not the real exchange rate but the kind of risks undertaken by the domestic financial system.

Either way, taxing capital flows is a suboptimal and indirect policy for dealing with these issues. If the problem is mostly from excessive expenditure during the boom phase, then the right policies are expenditure stabilization ones, possibly coupled with the development of foreign-exchange hedging strategies for the noncommodity export sector. If the problem is one of imprudence of the domestic financial system, then the issue is more one of domestic financial regulation and supervision than of capital-flows control.

In practice—as with the appreciation problems of Brazil, for example—the first policy that comes to mind is fiscal policy, not taxes on capital flows. The genesis of the appreciation problem in Brazil is at best 10 percent due to the second round of U.S. quantitative easing and 90 percent due to domestic fiscal policy and exorbitant local market interest rates. Hence, attacking capital inflows is really an avoidance strategy.

Similarly, the problems of the United States that led to the crisis did not have much to do with the level of capital inflows (and hence with the current-account deficits). Instead, the problem was the extreme bias of these flows toward AAA fixed-income assets, which interacted very poorly with incentives in the domestic financial system to create and hold assets that may have been AAA from the point of view of microeconomic shocks but not from the point of view of macroeconomic ones. Here again, the problem is one of inadequate capital charges for AAA collateralized debt obligation tranches and related assets, not capital inflows.

Some have argued that these structural problems cannot be fixed at the right speed and that we therefore cannot afford to let capital flows exacerbate their cost. I am sympathetic to this argument, but the complete argument must be made. Countries must explicitly say: "I have a serious problem here, and hence I have to slow down capital inflows while I fix the real problem." Absent this complete statement, policymakers may end up chasing symptoms rather than the illness.

Global Equilibrium Issues

The supply side must be looked at, as well. What is the responsibility of the countries that trigger the capital flows, either by maintaining large saving rates or by feeding carry trade by keeping funding costs very low?

I find this case even harder to make than the domestic justification for taxes on capital flows. What business is it of the United States, France, or Brazil to decide what is the optimal relative saving rate for China or of Greece and Portugal to decide the same for Germany? These high-saving countries have been a source of stability, not instability, for the world economy.

In industrial organization, we worry about low prices (in this case, low interest rates) when these are part of a deliberate strategy to destroy competition and hike prices later. Are we really worried that the Chinese are keeping rates low so that they later can punish the debtor countries by raising rates quickly? I doubt it.

The same applies to concerns about the effects of the second round of qualitative easing around the world. I do not see why the United States should risk a repeat of the Japanese lost decade because an overheating emerging market feels uneasy about it. By stabilizing U.S. equity markets, QE2 ended up doing just the opposite that was feared and reversed capital flows to emerging markets. Imposing our own preferences about macroeconomic policy frameworks on others is not likely to be effective, especially when we do not even understand the mechanisms.

Conclusion

When you run a fever, don't attack the thermometer. Deal with the real issues.

For emerging markets, the main concern at this time is a combination of making fiscal adjustment and fostering the development of domestic financial markets and foreign-exchange derivatives. Low interest rates are a fact of modern economic life, so we need to get used to them.

For developed economies, especially the United States, AAA assets that are created and held by banks need to have the appropriate capital charge if they are built on the basis of the law of large numbers and hence are exposed to systemic risk. The heavy demand for safe assets from the rest of the world will not abate, so we need to get used to that as well.

14

Remarks on Capital-Account Management and Other Macropolicy Topics

Arminio Fraga

The efficacy of capital controls is usually overestimated by governments and underestimated by market participants. Market players ignore the fact that governments may go way beyond optimal levels of taxes and controls, often because governments tend to ignore long-term costs and side effects. But if participants underestimate what governments may do, that is their problem. It does not matter.

More serious is what happens on the policy side. Policymakers see too little room for arbitrage, and therefore tend to ignore the loss of efficacy over time of most such policies. They also ignore or underestimate the side effects of controls.

Brazil's experience is a good example. For decades capital outflows from Brazil were banned. As a result, a black market for hard currency developed outside the boundaries of the law. Once money was taken out of the country, it could not be taxed. What is worse, this policy was part of the development of a culture of transgression, an integral part of the lost decade of 1981 to 1993. More recently, taxes on inflows have been introduced, but it is still too early to tell how relevant the side effects will be. The effects may include moving some portion of financial-market activity offshore, with loss of transparency and liquidity for locals, as well as a negative impact on more desirable long-term flows such as direct and equity investments.

This brings to mind a crucial point: the regulation of capital flows can be a useful tool, perhaps a second-best response. One very obvious example currently in evidence is the flood of short-term capital inflows to developing countries. However, while this is true, one must not forget that not all capital flows are driven by supply or push factors such as zero interest rates at the core of the system. Some may be driven by policies that themselves deliver undervalued exchange rates or ultra-high-interest rates in the recipient country, both key drivers of inflows.

So great care must be taken not to postpone or avoid facing more urgent problems. Again using Brazil as an example, nothing would do more for Brazil than policies that allowed interest rates to go down toward where they are in similar countries (say, 2 to 3 percent real rather than 6 percent real). This would greatly reduce the incentive for carry trades.

The same argument applies to China and Korea right now. In the case of China, one could argue that the pegging of the renminbi at an under-valued level is as much a bubble machine as the zero or close to zero interest rates found in the G3. All the money in the world wants to go to China.

More generally, we run the risk right now of seeing the widespread use of controls turn into a protectionist game, leading to large losses for the global economy in aggregate. Here there is a clear need for global coordination, as in the case of trade.

So what should countries do? Is there room for sensible capital controls? One conclusion that jumps to mind is that, in general, capital controls should not be seen as a permanent solution to problems.

Another key lesson, taught to us by Carlos Massad, a former governor of the Bank of Chile, is that policies that reduce volatility are good while policies that suppress volatility are bad.

The principles that apply to the ongoing debate on monetary and prudential policies apply to the case of capital account regulations and controls as well: risk is endogenous and systemic weaknesses must be addressed by macroprudential policies.

The most important case by far is the clear tendency for contemporary financial systems to generate way too much short-term borrowing in the aggregate. I do not believe this is a natural state of affairs but rather a man-made phenomenon, a creature of poorly designed incentives and asymmetric monetary policies, as mentioned by Otmar Issing. That must be fought by authorities at the root-cause level directly through the elimination of bad policies or through instruments such as the taxes suggested by Hyun Song Shin and others.

In a balance of payments context, the risk of allowing too much short-term borrowing tends to be amplified by the added currency mismatch, so there is an additional reason to watch out!

My conclusion is that capital account management tools should be applied in a context that is clearly prudential. They should not, however, be used to support undervalued currencies, in mercantilist fashion. Therefore, in practice this means capital account policies must be judged according to their objectives and not by the tools used in their implementation.

This brings me to a point that has been neglected in these times of zero rates, these times of push rather than pull: governments have a terrible track record of defending overvalued exchange rates. In my view they are likely to be just as bad in defending undervalued exchange rates. This poses two issues:

- At the country level, care must be taken to avoid creating credit and asset bubbles and losing control of inflation.
- At the International Monetary System level, the abuse of capital account tools can be just as damaging as protectionist policies, and can lead to the imbalances that we all know so well.

Lastly, I am of the view that central banks are perhaps being asked to do too much: to keep inflation low and stable, and to the extent possible to smooth the business cycle (not to try to abolish it); to be the financial regulator, with special emphasis on system risk; and, lastly, to manage the exchange rate.

The tools at the central bank's disposal are: monetary policy, prudential tools (reserve and margin requirements, taxes, etc.), and intervention in the foreign exchange market. The limitations of these tools and the short- and long-term constraints that these objectives must meet are reasonably well known, though not always by short-term-focused governments.

The central bank may also be called to the table to optimize the package with fiscal policy as an extra tool, adding an extra degree of complexity to the exercise. In theory, governments may deal with this difficult optimization problem in competent fashion. In practice, the challenges are tremendous, governments are rarely wise long-term optimizers, and problems and errors may easily ensue.

Take the case of intermediate exchange-rate regimes. I believe such regimes are possible, despite the time decay in the efficacy of capital account policies. I just don't think managed exchange rates are a good

idea. They lead to confusion and temptation. Confusion because economic actors are not given clear signals as to how they ought to structure
their economic and financial lives (e.g., their balance sheets) with respect
to interest-rate and exchange-rate risk. Temptation because governments
are often prone to succumb to short-term political pressures and end up
defending unsustainable exchange rates. My preference therefore is for
being closer to the extremes of the regime spectrum, allowing of course
room for prudential policies and, in the case of a flexible regime, for
intervention in exceptional circumstances.

Another important case has to do with fiscal policy. Many G3 countries are now running unsustainable budget deficits that in most cases
will tend to worsen over time. This approach is highly likely to end badly,
but no serious action is being taken yet.

Both of these examples belong in one form or another to the time-
consistency family. Great economic tragedies such as hyperinflations,
banking crises, and sovereign debt defaults, with their accompanying
social pain, are almost always the result of errors of this kind.

I therefore see great merit in the old-fashioned view of building sound
long-term institutional constraints, and in some degree of separation of
responsibilities. There is great frustration in the air concerning the
conduct of economic policies before and during the great financial crisis
of 2007 to 2009. This frustration is legitimate and provides great energy
to the ongoing effort to rethink policy frameworks and practices. But in
a world of fallible and short-term-focused policymaking, care must be
taken not to forget some important good old lessons and thus not to let
the pendulum swing too far toward excessive complexity and discretion.
In particular, I am of the view that a framework that delivers low and
stable inflation and sustainable fiscal policy is essential and must be
constructed where absent. Inflation targeting and fiscal responsibility
laws are a good way to achieve these goals. What is missing is a proper
macroprudential framework to supplement the always important (but
frequently flawed) microsupervision effort.

15

Capital-Account Management: Key Issues

Rakesh Mohan

The basic assumption in a lot of discussions about the capital account is that, in principle, the flow of capital across borders brings benefits to both capital importers and capital exporters. But historical evidence, reinforced by the current North Atlantic (not global) financial crisis that began in 2008, shows that it can create new exposures and bring new risks. In many emerging-market economies, financial or monetary stability has been compromised by the failure to understand and analyze such risks and by the excessive haste that many countries showed over time in liberalizing capital accounts. Such liberalization has usually been done without placing adequate prudential buffers that are needed to cope with the greater volatility characteristic of market-based capital movements. Such failure became manifest in the current crisis in a virulent form in the North Atlantic advanced economies.

In addressing issues related to capital-account management, I see them in the broader context of prudent macroeconomic and monetary management, with a focus on maintaining financial stability. Some of the errors in the approach to capital-account management arise from looking at it from the narrow viewpoint of capital controls. The reality of capital flows to emerging markets over the past decade and a half is one of rising volumes accompanied by high volatility. The optimal management of these large and volatile flows is not one-dimensional.

A combination of policies is needed:

- Sound macroeconomic policies, both fiscal and monetary,
- Exchange-rate flexibility with some degree of management,
- A relatively open capital account, but with some degree of management and controls,

- Prudent debt management,
- The use of macroprudential tools,
- Accumulation of appropriate levels of reserves as self-insurance and their symmetric use in the face of volatility in capital flows, and
- The development of resilient domestic financial markets.

That sounds like motherhood and apple pie, but capital-account management cannot be examined in isolation. It must be part of an overall toolkit with sound macroeconomic policies, both fiscal and monetary. Going to the extremes of total flexibility or fixed exchange rates needs to be avoided. Since the Asian crisis, emerging markets have practiced a greater degree of flexibility in exchange rates but with some degree of management. Similarly, emerging markets have maintained a relatively open capital account but, again, with some degree of management. The reality for Latin and Asian emerging-market economies has been somewhere in the middle over the past decade or so, as they avoided the extremes of the prevailing orthodoxy.

Appropriate levels of reserves need to be accumulated as self-insurance, and they can be used in the face of volatility in capital flows in a symmetric fashion—by injecting dollars into the market when there is a shortage of capital flows and doing the opposite when there are excess capital flows. That is what emerging-market countries have been doing since the Asian crisis.

Some propose that the way to cope with capital flows is to let the exchange rate appreciate. Further, volatility is said to be a problem because of the underdeveloped nature of domestic financial markets, which are inadequate for coping with such volatile capital flows, and so the answer really is to develop such capital markets. That is not the case.

With this kind of menu, there is no one size that fits all. The other part of this discussion that needs to be looked at is how to decide what to do, when, and to what extent.

Theory versus Practice

The guiding principle underlying most discussions on free capital mobility across borders is that it leads to more efficient allocation of resources and hence is welfare-enhancing to both borrowers and lenders. In principle, capital should flow from high-income capital-surplus countries to capital-scarce developing countries. But the reverse has been happening since the Asian crisis and particularly over the past decade. Capital has flowed from emerging-market economies to advanced economies. Free capital flows should lower the cost of capital in recipient countries and hence promote higher growth. They should be an important catalyst for a number of indirect benefits, such as development of domestic financial markets, improvements in local institutional development, and practice of better macroeconomic policies. If all these indirect benefits do indeed fructify, they should eventually show up in higher economic growth in the recipient countries.

What I find to be an enduring mystery in economic reasoning is that despite numerous cross-country studies that analyze the effects of capital-account liberalization, there is little evidence that capital-account liberalization enhances growth. In reviews of such studies, fewer than a quarter find any such relationship. It seems that economists in general do not like that result. They continue to insist that free cross-border capital flows are a good idea, despite their own empirical studies that do not give any evidence that there are such growth-enhancing benefits. And the studies that do find such evidence usually find it with a very mild effect. Yet the predominant view among economists and international policy advisers continues to be that open capital accounts are the first-best approach and that any form of capital-account management is decidedly a second-best one.

When any form of capital-account management or capital control is proposed, the reason given is that this has to be done because domestic financial markets are not developed enough, the implication being that when they are developed enough, such management will not be necessary. But is there evidence that developed and deep domestic financial markets are enough to withstand the kind of volatile capital flows that have been commonplace over the past decade? Such capital flows reached something like 10 percent of gross domestic product in India in 2007 and 2008. India did succeed in managing these flows in that period. We got battered and bruised in so doing but are still here to tell the tale!

The best clue to whether developed financial markets can cope with this comes from the interesting analysis provided by Ben S. Bernanke in a speech he gave at the Bank of France in February 2011 on the role of international capital flows in the current financial crisis in the United States. He recounted the various domestic and institutional factors that led to the U.S. crisis: "In addition to [these] domestic institutional factors, international capital flows likely played a significant role in helping to finance the housing bubble and thus set the stage for its subsequent bust" (Bernanke et al. 2011).

Bernanke analyzed the flows that came into the United States during the years before the crisis, both from official sources from what he calls the "emerging markets' global savings glut" and from largely private sources in Europe. He then concluded that "The United States, like some emerging-market economies during the 1990s, has learned that the interaction of strong capital flows and weaknesses in the domestic financial system can produce unintended and devastating results" (Bernanke et al. 2011).

But like most other economists, he went on to say that "The appropriate response is not to reverse financial globalization, which has considerable benefits overall. Rather, the United States must continue to work with its international partners to improve private-sector financial practices and strengthen financial regulation, including macroprudential oversight. The ultimate objective should be to be able to manage even larger flows of domestic and international capital" (Bernanke et al. 2011).

What can be learned from this? Even the most sophisticated, diversified, and deep financial market in the history of the world had weaknesses that inhibited it from absorbing large capital flows that came into the United States prior to the crisis. Stronger financial regulation and macroprudential oversight is required. This presumably applies to emerging markets even more strongly.

The Impossible Trinity

Much of the discussion on capital-account liberalization arises from belief in the impossible trinity, that the combination of an open capital account, a fixed exchange rate, and an independent monetary policy is not feasible. But since the Asian crisis, emerging-market economies in Latin America and in Asia have demonstrated that the "impossible" trinity can indeed be managed. They have realized that there is no need to be at the corners of the trinity. First, the exchange rate should be largely market-determined and flexible but still managed to a certain extent. Second, the capital account should be largely open but not fully open, with some degree of management including the exercise of controls. In such circumstances, the major emerging-market economies in Asia and Latin America survived the effects of the North Atlantic financial crisis without any financial institution in major Asian or Latin American countries getting into trouble. They have also demonstrated that by not being at the corners of the trinity, they can still manage or even practice independent monetary policy and have a certain degree of management of the capital account and a certain degree of management of the exchange rate. Most emerging-market economies have done exactly this. They also achieved during this period high growth, low inflation, and price and financial stability, which are things that we all want. We can go a little further and ask: Why do the emerging-market economies have to resort to this kind of policy mix?

The Need for Capital-Account Management

First, the record of capital volatility is stark over the last couple of decades. Prior to this decade, the previous peak of net capital flows to emerging-market economies was around U.S. $190 billion in 1995. The average over the four years prior to that was around $100 billion. There was a big reversal after the Asian crisis, but then these recovered to about $240 billion, on average, in 2003 to 2006. Net capital flows jumped to almost $700 billion in 2007 but then slumped to an average of around $200 billion during 2008 and 2009. That is the kind of capital-flow volatility that the emerging-market economies have experienced. So regarding the first point—why the emerging-market economies had to resort to this kind of management—it has indeed been due to the record of huge volatility in capital flows. It is a little difficult to imagine what would happen if capital-account management were not resorted to in active fashion in these countries.

Second, on average, there is a persistent inflation differential between advanced economies and emerging-market economies. In the ten or twelve years before the crisis, there was a persistent inflation differential of around 2 or 3 percent on average between advanced-economy inflation and emerging-market inflation, though with lots of variance between different counties. There was a persistent interest-rate differential as well, and that gave rise to huge opportunity for the carry trade on an enduring basis, since the differential has been persistent and is still continuing.

Third, there has been a good deal of volatility in the monetary policies of the advanced economies, and that has also given rise to capital-flow volatility. For thirty years, there has been broad correspondence between episodes of accommodative monetary policy in advanced economies and capital flows to emerging-market economies. And there has also been the reverse. Each tightening produced the reversal of capital flows and the crises that occurred in EMEs in the 1980s and 1990s. These episodes were well documented in the Committee on the Global Financial System's (CGFS) 2009 report on capital flows to EMEs.

Because the policies of advanced economies are driven by their own domestic needs, emerging markets need to take adequate defensive action. The growth differential has been getting starker. Overall, there is a huge incentive for high capital flows, which then lead to large exchange-rate appreciation, credit booms, and asset-price booms, followed eventually by higher trade and current-account deficits over time. There is then a reversal of capital flows at some point or other, leading to substantial output and unemployment costs. All of this could not have been managed by financial development, as shown by the United States itself. This demonstrates the need for a combination of measures, including capital management, particularly since markets can be irrational for extended periods.

Foreign-Exchange Reserves

A lot of discussion in recent years has centered on the large increases in foreign-exchange reserves of emerging-market economies. Most discussion focuses on the precautionary motive and on the search for rules that should govern the accumulation of such reserves.

The existence of substantive foreign-exchange reserves did cushion emerging-market economies from the significant reversal of capital flows that took place in 2008 and 2009 after the Lehman Brothers crisis. But it is difficult to know what level of reserves is adequate and to devise principles that can guide countries in their accumulation in the face of a rapidly changing and globalizing financial world.

What has not received adequate attention in this discussion is the need for expansion of central-bank balance sheets in the face of consistently high economic growth accompanied by financial deepening, which then requires corresponding growth in monetary aggregates. This requires expansion of base money (that is, the central-bank balance sheet) by an order of magnitude that is similar to that of financial growth, so there has been a continuous demand by the central banks of emerging markets for safe assets to add to their balance sheets. Such assets can be either safe domestic assets or foreign ones. If the country practices prudent macroeconomic and fiscal policy, the supply of domestic government securities may be inadequate to satisfy the central bank's demand for safe securities. In general, emerging-market economies exhibited high rates of economic growth over the past decade or so along with the practice of prudent macro and fiscal policies. Their central banks have exhibited a continuing demand for safe foreign assets, which the U.S. Treasury has obligingly supplied over this period, along with a large current-account deficit that also needed to be financed.

Apart from other reasons for the large accumulation of foreign-exchange reserves in recent years, there has been little discussion on this issue. An economy that is growing at around 15 percent annually in nominal terms while also undergoing associated financial deepening would typically need to expand the balance sheet of its central bank by a similar order of magnitude, which results in a growing and continuing demand for safe foreign assets. A good understanding of this motive for accumulating foreign-exchange reserves could lead to coordinated international policy action that addresses this need for safe assets by emerging-market economy central banks.

Conclusion

At least for emerging-market economies, capital-account management in its broad form should become part of the normal overall toolkit for macroeconomic management and be oriented toward ensuring growth with price and financial stability. It should not be regarded as a tool that is used only as an extreme measure. The accumulation and management of foreign-exchange reserves needs to be consistent with this overall approach.

References

Bernanke, Ben S., Carol Bertaut, Laurie DeMarco, and Steven Kamin. 2011. "International Capital Flows and the Returns to Safe Assets in the United States 2003–2007." *Banque de France Financial Stability Review* 15 (February): 13–26.

Committee on the Global Financial System. 2009. *Report of the Working Group on Capital Flows to Emerging Market Economies.* Basel: Bank for International Settlements (BIS).

16

The Case for Regulating Cross-Border Capital Flows

José Antonio Ocampo

Let me start this chapter with two remarks. The first one is that cross-border capital flows are one of the expressions of finance. It is thus peculiar that the Group of Twenty excluded this topic in its discussions about reregulating finance, as if cross-border finance were not finance. In fact, when we talk about regulating domestic finance, we always use the word *regulation*, but when we talk about cross-border finance, we use the word *controls*. I prefer and have long used the concept of capital-account regulations because they are regulations. Some are quantitative, such as the prohibitions on certain activities or limits on them, which is also true of some domestic prudential regulations. Some are price-based, such as unremunerated reserve requirements, again like domestic regulations, such as capital or liquidity requirements. They all belong to the same family of what we now call *macroprudential regulations*.

My second introductory point is that I come from a tradition of macroeconomic thinking in which the balance of payments is always placed at the center, as the source of both positive and negative shocks and therefore as the essential source of business cycles. This tradition is the best starting point to analyze the macroeconomic dynamics of developing countries and particularly of emerging-market economies. Furthermore, a broadly accepted principle is that the best policies are those designed to intervene directly at the source of the shocks. A clear case is a terms-of-trade shock. The best intervention in this case deals directly with the shock by saving a significant amount of a commodity price boom and using those savings later when prices fall. This is what Chile has been doing with its copper revenues and what Colombia did with coffee for a long time. This principle is widely accepted.

The same thing should be true of capital accounts. They are the main source of shocks that emerging markets have experienced in recent decades, both positive and negative. Therefore, policies should also focus in this case on the source of the shock. Furthermore, by referring to them as positive and negative, I am also expressing the fact that capital flows have a temporary component, which authorities may want to smooth out. Indeed, such smoothing out is the essence of what we mean by a countercyclical macroeconomic policy.

The starting point here is the recognition that finance is procyclical, particularly for those agents that are considered to be riskier by markets. This reflects the fact that there is a significant segmentation in financial markets and that riskier agents are subject to stronger procyclical shocks than the average market pattern. This is true of small and medium-sized enterprises and consumer credit in all economies. And it is true of developing countries in global markets. Developing countries are considered to be riskier borrowers, so they are subject to the phenomena of flight to quality and sudden stops during crises, but they are also subject to risk appetite during booms such as the one several emerging economies are experiencing now. That strong procyclicality is the particular issue that policies should address.

On top of that problem, in developing countries financial markets are more incomplete, and this is reflected in the variable mixes of currency and maturity mismatches in portfolios. These problems are more important for developing countries and emerging markets than they are for industrial economies. As countries develop deeper financial systems, markets will partly solve these problems. In any case, they should be the subject of specific attention by regulatory authorities.

Procyclicality is not only a question of short-term volatility. In a sense, short-term volatility is the easiest to administer through active foreign-exchange reserve management. The most difficult problem is managing the medium-term cycle of capital flows. We have experienced three such medium-term cycles in recent decades and may be starting a fourth. There was one that started in the mid-1970s and went through the 1980s. Then we had the 1990 to 1997 boom (briefly interrupted by the December 1994 Mexican crisis) and the long crisis that started in Asia in mid-1997. The most recent cycle was the boom from 2003 to mid-2008, followed by the sudden stop as a result of the Lehman

Brothers collapse. This was a shorter cycle, and a fourth one may have started in mid-2009.

The basic problem of these medium-term cycles is that they drive the macroeconomics of emerging and developing economies while simultaneously constraining the capacity to undertake countercyclical macroeconomic policies. They drive the exchange rate, spending, and domestic demand. They also drive fiscal policy in a procyclical way as revenues increase and access to capital markets is made easier during booms, and both are cut sharply during crises. They also drive interest rates in a procyclical way because markets tend to reduce risk spreads and thus interest rates during booms and increase them during crises. Therefore, countercyclical macroeconomic policy has to lean against those strong procyclical market trends. If authorities want to adopt countercyclical macroeconomic policies, they have to ask themselves why they would not want to intervene at all at the major source of the business cycle—the cyclicality of capital flows.

In fact, if authorities do not manage the capital account, they will really be making a choice about the particular way they want the procyclical effects of financial markets to be reflected in their economy. If they control the exchange rate, they will have to give up managing the interest rate, and then the policy package would be clearly procyclical. If they decide to control the interest rate, they have to give up managing the exchange rate, but appreciation during booms and depreciation during crises also have procyclical effects. The countercyclical effects that operate through the current account of the balance of payments are well known. But if we allowed this effect to run fully, exchange-rate appreciation during booms will tend to generate overvaluation and current-account deficits that increase the risk of a crisis later on. So it is a double-edged sword. Furthermore, procyclical effects operate through balance sheets in countries where the private sector has net external liabilities in foreign currencies and through income distribution (increases in real wages as a result of appreciation and reductions due to depreciation). These procyclical effects tend to predominate in practice.

In both cases, authorities are not controlling procyclicality: they are really choosing which effect of market procyclicality they are allowing into the economy. This looks very much more like Robert Mundell's analysis of a fixed exchange-rate system: authorities control the composition of the quantity of money, but they have no control over the quantity of money. In the case we are discussing, authorities are choosing whether they want the procyclicality of global financial markets to be reflected in interest rates or exchange rates, but they are not controlling procyclicality. That is why, if authorities are thinking of doing countercyclical management, they should start by looking at the source of procyclicality—the capital account. And they will have to think of combining this with aggressive foreign-exchange reserve management. One way of understanding this is that, since the instruments they normally have are insufficient to run a countercyclical policy, they have to look for additional ones.

The developing-country and emerging-market authorities have actually been quite wise in this regard. They have discovered that they can obtain more degrees of freedom to adopt countercyclical macroeconomic policies by adding policy instruments, either intervening massively in the foreign-exchange market (buying and selling depending on the phase of the cycle) or regulating capital flows—or both. In this regard, I agree with a point that Rakesh Mohan has raised about the impossible trinity being a somewhat confusing way of understanding the policy choices (chapter 15 in this book). In fact, all the interesting things happen inside the impossible trinity.

What does the empirical work on the effectiveness of regulations of the capital account indicate? The most comprehensive analysis I have read on this issue is a 2000 International Monetary Fund study by Akira Ariyoshi and others. The one that was done in 2010 by Jonathan Ostry and collaborators was provocative and an excellent way to stimulate the appetite for the debate, but I think the IMF should take a broader look at what countries experience and what those experiences reveal about the effectiveness of different types of regulations.

Considering those studies and many others, capital-account regulations can be said to have two different effects. The first effect is that they operate as a liability policy. They are designed to improve the term structure of the country's liabilities, and in this regard, the evidence is strong that regulations are effective, whether they are price- or quantity-based.

The second effect is that regulations are a complement or support to countercyclical macroeconomic policies. In this regard, the evidence has been subject to much more debate, particularly in the case of price-based controls, such as the unremunerated reserve requirements used by Chile and Colombia in the 1990s and Colombia again in the mid-2000s. Studies have shown, however, that they affect the quantity of flows or domestic interest rates or both, thus allowing authorities to increase rates during booms without attracting additional capital flows. Either way, they are effective, and monetary policy will then determine whether the regulations affect the quantity of flows or the domestic interest rate or a mix of both. Regulations are effective as long as the margin between the domestic interest rate and the foreign interest rate can be raised without attracting additional capital flows or as long as flows can be reduced at given interest-rate differentials.

The evidence also indicates that some of those effects are temporary. In my writings, I have referred to capital-account regulations as speed bumps rather than permanent restrictions because market agents learn how to avoid them. This implies that authorities have to be equally dynamic, strengthen regulations over time, and close loopholes to make them effective. This is true for any type of prudential regulation. Authorities always have to see how the market is evolving and adjust regulations to make them more effective.

V

Growth Strategies

Questions: How Should the Crisis Affect Our Views of Growth and Growth Strategies?

Income Distribution and Growth

The economic crisis that began in 2008 was preceded by a long period of high growth and rising income inequality. This was true in both advanced countries and emerging-market countries. The distribution of wages widened. The share of profits increased. The share of income going to the top 1 percent increased even more.

These patterns raise important and well-understood issues of equity. They also potentially raise issues of efficiency. Some argue that the increase in income inequality was at the source of the large decrease in household saving in the United States as people tried to maintain consumption growth by borrowing. Some argue that the emergence of a middle class in China is essential to the development of more advanced products where technological progress is higher.

If the diagnosis is correct, can the problem be handled through conventional policies, or does it require a more dramatic reassessment of the growth model and of institutions?

Catch-Up, Export-Led Growth, and Industrial Policy

Precrisis, countries far from the technology frontier were catching up with those at the frontier. Growth rates were much higher in emerging-market countries than in advanced countries. This is clearly a desirable development, but it raises a number of issues.

Many emerging-market countries followed an export-led growth strategy—a low exchange rate, associated with low domestic demand; a large manufacturing sector, associated with technology transfer; and high productivity growth. The strategy has worked well in many countries. Should they continue or shift to domestic demand? Should they be allowed to continue? Or should it be seen as a form of unfair competition and treated as such? Are there ways of following a similar strategy without running large current-account surpluses (along the lines of Dani Rodrik's work)?

Some advanced economies, especially in Europe, are experiencing very low growth. Most of them are close to or at the technology frontier. Can their growth rates be substantially increased?

In 2004, Paul Samuelson argued that technology transfer could make advanced countries strictly poorer. The argument was largely dismissed by trade economists on the grounds that it implied a decrease in trade, which we have not observed. Could it be that the effect, although not dominating now, is present and even increasing in strength, with important implications for growth in advanced countries?

Industrial Policy and Growth

One lesson that has been learned from the crisis is that unfettered markets do not always work best. In many countries, there is increasing talk of industrial policy. Should we revise our views about the pros and cons of industrial policy (for example, along the lines advocated by Philippe Aghion)? How does the case for industrial policy depend on how far a country is from the technology frontier?

Institutions and Growth

Emerging countries have generally done better than advanced countries in the current crisis. After suffering a sharp decline in trade and, in many cases, sharp outflows, they have returned to growth and, in some cases, to their precrisis output path. Conventional wisdom is that they had better institutions (in part, due to the lessons from past crises) and better fiscal policy (better than in the past but better than advanced countries?). Are these the sources of their better performance? Was the extent of financial integration relevant to the outcome?

Financial Liberalization and Growth

The crisis has shown the tradeoff from financial liberalization—more efficient intermediation but higher risk. If we take it as given that regulation will always remain one step behind financial innovation, should we revisit the benefits and costs of financial liberalization and of financial openness for growth?

17

Do We Need to Rethink Growth Policies?

Dani Rodrik

The current economic crisis has taught us new things, but it does not require a complete rethinking of what we know about growth. The main new thing is that the context in which we are going to think about growth policies might be different. The context arises partly from the difficulties that the advanced countries are going to be facing with the debt overhang and possibly lower growth. What does that do to the growth prospects of the developing countries?

As we go forward, there are doubts about the system for cross-border financial flows, and there is a systemic worry about whether we are moving toward a world without a leader or without leadership where it will be difficult to sustain global cooperation.

One issue that is overlooked in discussions on growth is that the fundamental force that is driving growth in developing countries is convergence. There is a large gap between potential output (provided by the technology levels that already exist in the advanced countries) and actual output (based on the technology that developing countries currently have), and this gap drives development.

Another issue that is overlooked in discussions on growth is that this potential must be achieved rather than take place automatically. In other words, convergence is conditional. It is not automatic. It is going to depend on the things that economies do and get right.

The point about growth depending on convergence is important because it puts the focus on the supply side of things—on what countries do to absorb those technologies—and it downplays the demand side. Much of the discussion about growth is about whether developing countries can grow rapidly when the advanced countries are unable to. But regardless of how rapidly the rich countries grow, the convergence gap is still there. In fact, it is bigger than it has been in a long time.

To a first order of approximation, over the medium term the growth rate of the rich countries is largely irrelevant to the question of how much growth can occur in the developing and emerging markets. In other words, how rapidly the frontier is moving is of second-order importance relative to the gap between where the frontier is and where the poor countries are.

The bad news is that since convergence is conditional, it depends on policymakers' having a good handle on what the right policies in the developing world are. Here there have been a succession of various "consensuses," and now the consensus is perhaps best represented by *The Growth Report: Strategies for Sustained Growth and Inclusive Development*, which Michael Spence put together for the Commission on Growth and Development (December 2010). It is a consensus about pragmatism and about search and about context specificity and appropriate policies. It moves the discussion away from a list of specific dos and don'ts that were economists' focus a decade or so ago.

Prior to the crisis, developing countries were growing rapidly, so one question is, "What does that rapid growth tell us about what is likely to happen in the future, and is that growth sustainable?" Much of the growth of Latin America and Sub-Saharan Africa prior to the crisis was misleading because they had experienced a long period of lagging behind and were making up for lost ground. On the other hand, that also means that the convergence gap between those parts of the world and the advanced countries is actually wider than at any time since the 1970s (figure 17.1).

In figure 17.1, consider the ratio of per capita income in Latin America as a share of per capita income in the rich part of the world. The last decade in Latin America shows the process of convergence, but still the convergence gap between the average income levels in Latin America and in rich countries is wider now than what it has been since the 1970s. The ultimate dynamic, the potential for growth and catch-up and convergence, is larger now than at any time before.

That is also true for Sub-Saharan Africa, which experienced rapid growth in the last decade or so. But as you can see from the figure, relative to the frontier it is far below where the continent was earlier. Only

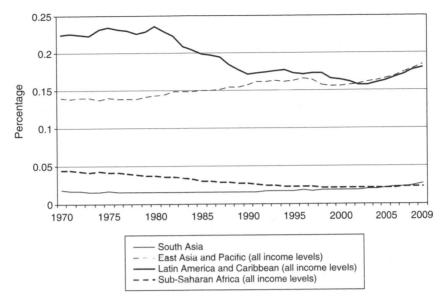

Figure 17.1
A wider convergence gap (for most): Incomes as a ratio of high-income countries.

Asia experienced sustained convergence in this period, so Asia is where the convergence gap has diminished.

What is convergence conditional on? What are its prerequisites? Here I develop the half of the argument that is relevant for this discussion. The economic component of convergence is a process of ongoing structural transformation. A lot of the growth in the developing world takes place through the creation of new industries at higher productivity levels and through a transfer of resources within those economies from the lower-productivity activities to the higher-productivity activities.

Tradables, particularly modern tradable industries, play an important role globally, and therefore safeguarding the health of modern tradable economic activities, monitoring the exchange rate, and enacting policies that promote tradables become important. From this perspective, a certain amount of financial deglobalization may not be bad news for developing and emerging markets because it allows them to maintain exchange rates that might be more competitive than would be the case otherwise.

The other thing that has been learned about the process of convergence is that sometimes we get the short-term economics right but we also need to get the medium-term politics right. The medium-term politics is really the building up of institutions of conflict management. Economies are consistently buffeted by a variety of internal and external shocks, and the ability to handle those shocks and bring about the macroeconomic and policy adjustments that those shocks require is a key determinant of whether growth spurts fizzle out. The key is whether domestic politics allows the appropriate responses to the shocks, and it is this that determines whether countries are able to engineer a succession of growth accelerations or experience only short-term growth that soon fades.

As economists, we have more to say on structural transformation, so I want to spend more time on it. An old concept in development economics is dualism, and this remains a key feature in the developing world. Developing countries have a mix of high-productivity and low-productivity activities, with large gaps in productivity levels across these activities. Consider the relationship between a measure of dispersion of labor productivity across different sectors of an economy and the level of development of that economy (figure 17.2). As the average level of labor productivity in an economy rises, intersectoral productivity gaps tend to shrink, approaching those of the rich economies. In the poor and middle-income economies, there are large gaps in labor productivity.[1]

The key implication of the structural transformation imperative from a policy perspective is that while the composition of output may be of second-order importance in a rich country, it is of first-order importance for economic performance and economic growth in a developing country. It is crucial for developing countries to achieve the right mix of economic activities.

Figure 17.3 compares agriculture's labor productivity to productivity in the rest of the economy and shows what happens to this ratio over the course of development. There is a universal U-shaped relationship: the relative productivity of agriculture first falls and then rises. First, at very low levels of development, new industries need to arise. When a country is starting from a very low level of development, everybody works in agriculture, and there is no industry, so agricultural productivity is the same as productivity in the rest of the economy. Growth begins

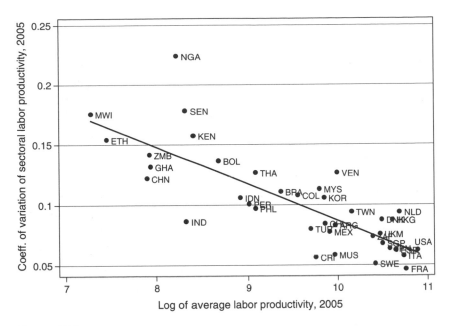

Figure 17.2
Large productivity gaps in developing countries: The relationship between inter-sectoral productivity gaps and income levels.

when new industries start developing, and therefore the relative productivity of agriculture starts to fall.

This is the first dynamic, but over time, people shift from agriculture into the more modern parts of the economy. This drives the process of convergence within the economy, and the relative productivity of agriculture starts to catch up with that of the rest of the economy. Both dynamics are needed—new industries and a process of ongoing transformation (ongoing movement of labor and other resources from the old to the new). This is not much different from Sir Arthur Lewis's model of dualism, where there is a quasi-automatic movement of workers from traditional industries to modern industries.

One of the most surprising things that I have seen in the last few decades is that in large parts of the world today, structural transformation is taking place in reverse. People are moving from high-productivity activities to low-productivity activities and not the other way around. Figure 17.4 shows the decomposition of overall labor-productivity growth in different parts of the world across different sectors. The light

(a)

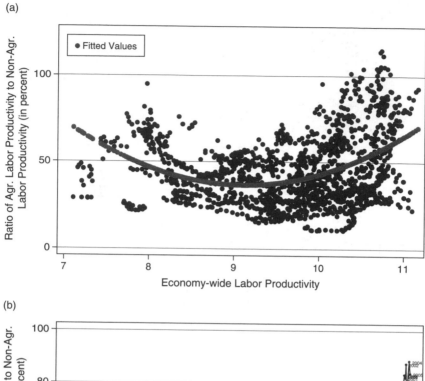

(b)

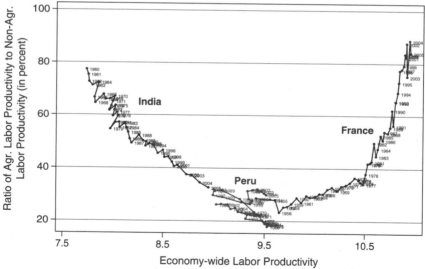

Figure 17.3
Growth from both new activities and ongoing structural change: The relationship between economywide labor productivity (horizontal axis) and the ratio of agricultural productivity to nonagricultural productivity (vertical axis).

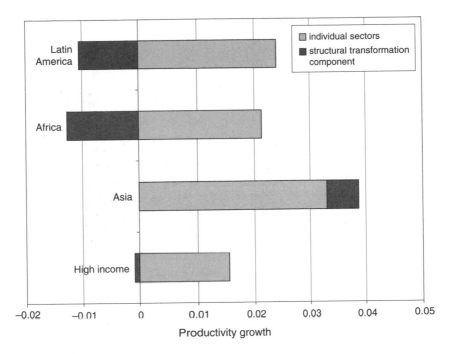

Figure 17.4
Growth-enhancing structural transformation is not automatic: The decomposition of productivity growth by country group, 1990 to 2005.

gray bar shows labor productivity growth on average within individual sectors. The dark gray bar shows how the reallocation of labor across different sectors has affected economywide labor-productivity growth—the structural transformation component.

In figure 17.4, Asia behaves in the way that all developing countries would be expected to behave. In China, India, and Thailand, labor is moving from agriculture and other low-productivity activities to high-productivity activities. But for the same period, growth-reducing structural change is taking place in Africa and Latin America. One explanation is that manufacturing is shrinking and informality is expanding. This is a part of the picture that we have missed by looking, for example, at how successful export-oriented manufacturing has become in Latin America. We have forgotten to ask what happens to the workers who are displaced from these firms that become more productive by rationalizing production, upgrading technology, and substituting capital for labor. These workers end up not in more productive activities but in less productive activities.

In the high-income countries, there are not large gaps in productivity, and therefore the intersectoral component is not large in that group of countries. Reversing this perverse outcome is critical if emerging markets in Latin America and Africa are going to generate ongoing sustained growth based on desirable structural transformation rather than based on high commodity prices or short-term capital-inflow-driven growth spurts (figure 17.5).

A couple of things seem to lie behind helping to drive this distinction between countries that are experiencing the right kind of structural change versus countries that are not. A country's initial comparative advantage matters a lot. A country that starts out with a comparative advantage in natural resources and in primary products and that globalizes based on that comparative advantage specializes in activities that cannot absorb a lot of labor. Those kinds of growth models are not generating a lot of employment in the more productive parts of the economy. In other words, integrating into a world economy with a comparative advantage in natural resources is not conducive to the kind of structural change that drives long-term sustained growth (figure 17.6).

But there are indications that the natural resources "disadvantage" can be offset with various policies. One policy is, once again, the exchange rate. Countries that have competitive exchange rates have more desirable structural change. Overvaluation is the enemy of growth-increasing structural change, and undervaluation is a help to achieving it. A second policy worth considering is labor-market policy. Countries with more flexible labor markets appear to be better at promoting structural growth and at increasing structural change than other countries are (figure 17.7).

In conclusion, let me connect this perspective on growth with some of the systemic issues that I started with. First, the discussion should not be about which countries will be the growth engine of the world and whether developing-country growth will be adversely affected by low growth in the rich countries. This is a demand-driven, short-term perspective on growth and it is not the right way to think about medium- to long-term growth in the developing countries. The drivers of growth need to be analyzed from the supply side, and from the perspective of the

(a)

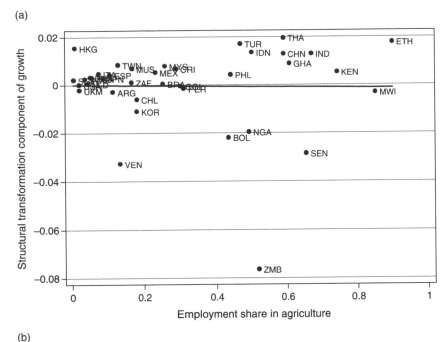

(b)

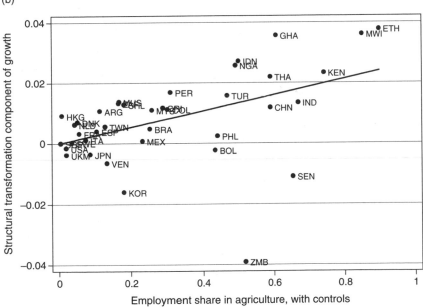

Figure 17.5
Conditional help from a large reservoir of excess labor: The association between the initial labor share in agriculture and the contribution of structural change to growth.

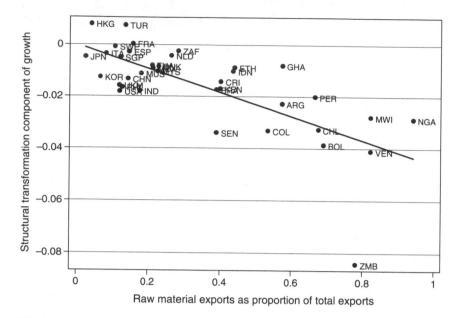

Figure 17.6
The bad news of a comparative advantage in primary products: The partial association between the share of primary products in exports and the contribution of structural change to growth.

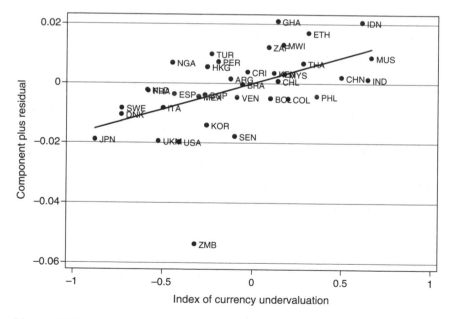

Figure 17.7
Help from policy: The partial association between an index of currency undervaluation and the contribution of structural change to growth.

mechanisms of engines of growth within the developing countries. That engine is structural change within the developing world, a process that is fraught with difficulties and requires policy support.

From the standpoint of multilateral institutions, the policy environment for developing countries needs to leave room for pursuing the appropriate structural transformation policies and for pursuing policies with the kinds of instruments that have the least adverse spillovers on the rest of the world. Developing countries need to have access to the policies that will help them change the composition of output and do it with the least amount of external spillovers.

The greatest failure here has been China and global imbalances. China has changed its composition of output through undervaluation policies that have spilled over into its external surplus. In principle, you can achieve the transformation of output that you need not through exchange-rate macropolicies but through sectoral microeconomic policies. That is, you can achieve transformation through trade and industrial policies that have direct effects on the structure of output and production (i.e., policies that alter relative prices) without altering the relationship between income and expenditure or the external balance. The international environment has pushed China to pursue the wrong kinds of policies. It has prevented China from using its trade and industrial policies because there is much greater discipline in the World Trade Organization on trade and industrial policies than on exchange rates.

Instead we need to move to a world where we have much greater discipline on currency policies because these create first-order spillovers across countries. Correspondingly, we also should have less discipline over trade and industrial policies so that we can reconcile the need for structural transformation in the developing world with the need to minimize macroeconomic imbalances.

Note

1. These and the subsequent results on structural transformation I discuss below are taken from my work with Maggie McMillan. See Margaret S. McMillan and Dani Rodrik, "Globalization, Structural Change, and Economic Growth," National Bureau of Economic Research Working Paper 17143, National Bureau of Economic Research, Cambridge, MA, June 2011.

18

Is the Chinese Growth Model Replicable?

Andrew Sheng

Although I refer to the Chinese growth model in this chapter, I am really talking about the Asian growth model more generally. The real issue is that the global financial crisis that began in 2008 has challenged our thinking about growth, equity distribution, industrial policy, and the role of the markets. Going forward, we are facing both a financial crisis and a global climate-change crisis. One is immediate, the other one is longer term, but both have the same origin—excess consumption financed by excess leverage.

Crises seem to occur every ten years. Twenty years ago, it was the failure of the Soviet system, which had no hard budget constraint. My contention is that the present financial capital market has no hard budget constraint. The banking system can leverage itself to whatever size possible, and when banks fail, the losses are underwritten by the state. So there are similarities regarding this problem.

Regarding the problem of institutions that are too big to fail: when does finance leverage itself in a way that moves it into a predatory algorithm? We do not have academic answers for this question. We do not even have a practical answer to this hard-budget-constraint issue. This is not a regulatory issue. Regulatory reforms cannot deal with this problem. This is a political problem that we have not solved.

We are facing a global climate-change problem, and the real issue is that if people in the developing countries live the lifestyle of those in the advanced countries, then there will be no natural resources left. The average Chinese and Indian cannot live the average American way of life without destroying the world's natural resources. If all five billion people in the emerging markets start living the life of the average American and consume the same amount of natural resources per capita, then we will have a global crisis on our hands.

Changing lifestyles is a major problem that needs to be addressed. Emerging markets also need to shift from an export-driven model of growth to domestic consumption–led growth. These are the critical issues.

Growth models have moved from ideal policies (what is good and what is bad) to a more practical standard—namely, what works. We have also seen the mistakes of monoculture. If we have one standard for the whole world and if that standard is wrong, then the whole world pays for it. Diversity is important, and differences of view are important.

The crucial problems are information asymmetry and agency problems. Fragmented academic disciplines and fragmented bureaucratic structures are preventing us from seeing a systemic problem, and this crisis is a systemic problem. If we see only part of the problem and the part we see is somebody else's problem, then we have global markets but national regulations, and national policies do not add up at the global level. Everybody says it is everybody else's problem, but it is actually a systemic issue.

Another problem is that if finance—the agent of growth and development, the agent of fiduciary trust—becomes five times larger (in assets) than global gross domestic product, then it is no longer an agent. It is a principal. Proprietary trading is about finance acting on its own behalf, not on behalf of the real sector.

Was the Asian growth model wrong? There was an Asian crisis, and the model needed to be modified. But the Asian model appears to be successful, although it is less elegant in its ability to explain itself. After the Asian crisis, Asia moved to become a self-insured, adaptive-growth, supply-chain model. This was essentially invented by the Japanese when they adopted Henry Ford's assembly line, added just-in-time inventory management, expanded the supply chain to include clusters of suppliers, and then extended that supply chain to the Four Dragons and then the Four Tigers. Today that supply chain is in China, India, and Vietnam and has become global.

Supply chains are networks, and financial markets are networks. In this global network system, there are fragmented national laws and national thinking. Growth is about adapting global experience and practices to local conditions. That is innovation. The concept of the global supply chain now is accepted in the business community, but it is rarely used by economists. The World Bank, however, is thinking about cities and geographical space and the Coasian reduction of transactions costs. All of these are essentially about networks and supply chains.

Some have asked whether the Chinese model can be replicated. Barry Naughton, who looks closely at Chinese state enterprises and growth, has written about this singularity versus replicability issue. He claims that China has so many unique features that its successes are not replicable but that some process innovations in China can provide lessons about the nature of institutions and interactions between institutions in the development process.

I think that his intuition is right but that the Chinese growth model is actually about the process of growth. The problem with the Washington Consensus was that it confused an ideal with the journey of reaching that ideal. That journey has huge information asymmetry. How can you form rules, as Paul Romer says, when nobody knows what that rule is? If we have gone to a path where nobody understands what this unknown unknown is all about, can you have rules? Can you formulate the proper rules if you do not understand what is going on? The only way you can proceed is to move pragmatically on a search-and-experiment basis. It is all about networks, markets, and adaptive systems. The Western theory of complex adaptive systems is a good way of explaining Chinese and Asian growth. Policies such as capital adequacy, capital models, and export models are not being used, but the growth model is seen as an adaptive system within a global system. And the Chinese actually work on this on a pragmatic basis.

Influential books about growth in China—such as Angeline G. Chen's *Taiwan's International Personality: Crossing the River by Feeling the Stones* (1998) and Robert Weil's *Red Cat, White Cat: China and the Contradictions of "Market Socialism"* (1996)—treat the Chinese model as if it were idiosyncratic and not replicable. The real issue is that in a common law system, microrules are decided by magistrates and judges until an issue develops into a common law principle. China is very much administrative, but it also accumulates small rules into major policy decisions (at the highest level). What matters is orchestration—building the national supply chain and the linkages with the global supply chain.

According to Thomas J. Peters, tight policies are followed by organizations that have a clear vision of where they want to go. One of China's tight policies was Deng Xiaoping's 1979 Four Modernizations—modernize agriculture, modernize industry, modernize defense, and modernize science and technology. But because workers had never before tried to accomplish these modernizations, they needed very tight decision rules. What decision rules? As early as 1962, Deng was quoting a Sichuan proverb: "No matter if it is a black cat or a white cat; as long as it can catch mice, it is a good cat." As long as it works, do it. So it is about practice, not theory. It is about experimentation and open-mindedness.

The middle stage is more complex. It requires looseness. The supply chain can be foreign owned, locally owned, or state owned. As long as it works, you follow that supply chain. This approach was not invented in China. The Chinese and Koreans copied it from the Japanese, and the Japanese copied the idea from the Americans. Everybody is learning and adapting. The competition within China is between cities, and it is about adapting these supply chains.

The Chinese innovation in this process is that the government can assist a private-sector supply chain by implementing rules, infrastructure, and telecommunications—rather than adding transaction costs that increase supply-chain inefficiencies. China integrated its small and medium-sized enterprises (SMEs) and multinational corporations into the global supply chain. The growth strategy becomes one of picking a supply chain—abandon a dead or closed supply chain and invest in a successful supply chain.

This approach has resulted in a pragmatic, adaptive system. Partly because of the advantages of scale, China has evolved special market cities where the state reduces the transactions costs of SMEs and enables them to join the multinational supply chain. Competition today is no longer one of company versus company or nation versus nation. It is about supply chain versus supply chain, and that supply chain is cross-national, not just Chinese.

In China, a large part of that supply chain is actually owned by foreigners. The challenge for this multinational supply chain is that it requires orchestration to bridge the differences between the old authoritarian model and the current free-market model. In an orchestra, the players cannot be free to play whatever they wish to play, and the conductor cannot overwhelm the musical score with idiosyncratic interpretations of the notes. Feedback mechanisms are needed between the conductor and the players.

The current regulatory system of free markets assumes that if every single player is safe or if every single player is a very good player, then they will produce good music. But this is not inevitable or preordained. A good musical outcome requires a productive relationship between the conductor and the orchestra and a context in which the orchestra can move to make good music. The resulting music depends partly on the musicians and partly on the conductor. Likewise, in the relationship between the supply chain and the state, the state learns how to play with good feedback mechanisms to gauge whether the system is working and to create that growth model.

The model requires an interactive feedback mechanism between the conductor/state and the players/market. This is not an either/or situation in which either the state controls everything or the free market requires everything to be market-based, with minimal government involvement. It is about encouraging the proper feedback mechanisms between the state and the market, including the global market, to ensure that the overall supply chain operates smoothly.

In conclusion, growth as a process is replicable. There are no ideal policies that are optimal. As we all cross rivers by feeling the stones, we are finding that the stones in each river are different and that the distance between one river and the shore is also different from the distance between another river and the shore. Complex adaptive systems are needed, and often there is no difference between macro and micro. The macro depends on the micro, the micro depends on the macro, and the aggregate micro does not necessarily add up to a macro. We need to understand the interactive actions between them.

References

Chen, Angeline G. 1998. "Taiwan's International Personality: Crossing the River by Feeling the Stones." *Loyola of Los Angeles International and Comparative Law Review* 20 (223).

Naughton, Barry. 2009. "Singularity and Replicability in China's Development Experience." Presented to the American Economics Association Meeting, San Francisco.

Romer, Paul. 1990. "Endogenous Technological Change." *Journal of Political Economy* 98 (5):S71–S102.

Weil, Robert. 1996. *Red Cat, White Cat: China and the Contradictions of "Market Socialism."* New York: Monthly Review Press.

19
Growth in the Postcrisis World

Michael Spence

Macroeconomic Stability

Before the crisis of 2008, macroeconomic stability was correctly perceived as a necessary but not sufficient condition for sustained growth. There were muted business cycles, shocks, and asset bubbles in the advanced economies but not really bouts of instability that threatened the balance of these economies. Macroeconomic instability was viewed mainly as a challenge in developing economies. The crisis turned this thinking on its head.

Postcrisis, we no longer take macroeconomic stability for granted and must rethink the proposition that emerging economies are inherently more prone to instability than the advanced ones. But the necessary condition remains true, and the principal challenge is how to achieve it, domestically and in the global economy. Interdependence and the increasing size of the emerging economies as a group imply that instability and crises originating in one part impair potential economic performance everywhere.

Most of the discussion is devoted to policy and policy frameworks. Policy in several categories is important and needs to be rethought, but it is a mistake to focus exclusively on policy. A critical ingredient in creating the recent crisis was the inability of the participants, both regulators and private-sector participants, to perceive risk accurately. The conceptual frameworks for assessing the dynamics of risk proved inadequate. As a result, the presumed self-regulatory properties of the system evidently failed, contributing to the crisis. One conclusion is clear. As part of the effort to improve the system, we need to recognize that the models of risk in the financial system are incomplete. It is a challenge and an opportunity for those in the academic community, among others.

I do not agree that the self-regulatory properties should always be presumed to be missing and that the burden falls on regulation. It seems unwise to assume the conclusion in advance. New and better models of the dynamics of risk will influence the behavior of investors and intermediaries. The recognition that the models are incomplete already has.

Let me turn now to growth dynamics. In advanced countries, long-run growth is driven by innovation and growth in the labor force. Capital deepening has its limits, as Robert Solow's work showed. Emerging economies have the following principal ingredients of sustained high growth:

- Macroeconomic stability
- Engagement with the global economy
- Inbound knowledge transfer
- Export diversification and structural change
- Capital deepening (Investment rates are in the range of 25 to 35 percent of gross domestic product, including public-sector investment rates in the range of 5 to 7 percent of GDP. With capital to output ratios in the range of 2.5 to 3.3, these investment rates support growth in the 7 to 10 percent range.)
- High rates of public-sector investment (These raise the return to private-sector investment, including foreign direct investment, and hence the level of the latter.)
- Inclusiveness in employment opportunities and access to education
- Policy setting that involves decisions made under uncertainty with incomplete models and that has a pragmatic and experimental component

This is a short summary. A fuller treatment can be found in the Commission on Growth and Development's *The Growth Report: Strategies for Sustained Growth and Inclusive Development* (December 2010) (see also my 2011 book, *The Next Convergence: The Future of Economic Growth in a Multispeed World*).

In the future, there will be additional longer-term issues. They can be thought of as a collection of problems that represent a challenge to the replicability and sustainability of the model that focused on an individual developing economy and that presumed that the global economy was large in relation to it.

An interesting and recent development is a growing recognition in the large emerging economies that the growth paths of their predecessors and the advanced countries will not work because they put too much strain on natural resources and the environment. They are at the beginning of embarking on a new growth path that will involve different patterns of energy consumption, urban density, transportation modes and investment, and much more. Their aggregate projected economic size dictates that they take an alternative course, regardless of the paths that advanced countries follow. Projecting out into the future, these countries will account for well over 60 percent of global GDP, and China and India, which will lead the shift, will be individually large. In the language of economics, the incentives will be to a great extent internalized, and the free-rider problem will be less daunting.

Turning to the crisis that began in 2008, there was some concern in developing countries that the crisis would be misinterpreted as a broad failure of a market-driven capitalist approach to growth, with the result that it would be rejected, notwithstanding past success, and replaced by a more inward-looking, state-centric, and interventionist approach. The argument would be that the global economy is too unstable and dangerous. The financial system, at least, is less stable than most thought. But by and large, this shifting of strategy and direction has not happened, perhaps because the recovery in the major emerging markets was rapid. The crisis is now pretty much universally viewed as a failure of the advanced-country financial systems, with supporting trends in the global economy that contributed to disguising the growing instability.

Nevertheless, lessons have been learned, but they are too numerous to deal with in detail here. By way of summary, the importance of initial conditions and conservative positioning prior to a crisis (a set of lessons learned in 1997 and 1998) was reinforced by this crisis. The 2008 crisis and the commodity-price spike that preceded it also brought to the forefront the importance of paying attention to distributional issues, across households and businesses. More attention is now being paid to prebuilt mechanisms that can be rapidly deployed to counter the adverse income, employment, and credit effects of crises.

In the past twenty years, some areas of policies have generated a diversity of views and practice. There has been some convergence of views, but it is certainly incomplete. The major areas that have this kind of diversity are (1) industrial- and export-diversification policy, (2) the pace and sequencing of opening up the current account (an area influenced by the World Trade Organization's rules and negotiations), and (3) the capital account, particularly the use and misuse of capital controls on various types of cross-border capital flows and reserve accumulation. On one level, the crisis has not substantially changed the positioning, but there has been some shift. The importance of a domestically owned component of the banking system is now widely understood. The credibility of the open capital-account position (pushed before the crisis of 1997 and 1998 and then modified somewhat in the aftermath) was further reduced by unexpected instability in the advanced-country financial systems and by the need to take defensive action against rapid capital outflows and to offset the effects of large inflows (particularly inflation, asset-price bubbles, and rapid appreciation of the currency). On balance, the crisis has reinforced the pragmatic, somewhat gradual, step-by-step approach, without negating the risks of extended over- or undervaluation. The risks of these two are asymmetric and quite different with respect to timing. Valuation is less well understood. Eventually, it achieves its negative effect by damaging the incentives for structural transformation of the economy and hence the underpinnings of growth.

The current crisis hit developing countries through two channels. One was the rapid exodus of capital and a resultant credit tightening, combined with downward pressure on the currency. The second was a precipitous drop in trade and hence aggregate demand. On the credit side, central banks moved quickly and in collaboration with domestic financial institutions, preventing a drying up of credit. Reserves were used to moderate the pace of net capital outflows on the private side of the current account. Collaboration among central banks was significant and important. On the trade side, there was no place to hide. Countries varied in their capacity for fiscal stimulus and used whatever capacity they had. China, with the largest capacity, used it in the form of a two-year stimulus program amounting to 9 percent of GDP a year and combined it with a rapid and dramatic easing of credit that has left some residual problems, which probably are manageable. With the help of a rapid bounce back in trade, including among the major emerging markets, and these policy responses, emerging economies bounced back and experienced the V-shaped recovery that was hoped for and to some extent mistakenly expected in the advanced countries, where balance-sheet damage in the financial and household sectors was much greater. The recovery in terms of magnitude and speed came in China, India, and Brazil, in that order. This rapid recovery has given the emerging economies a greater sense of resilience and confidence, and rightly so.

The effectiveness of the crisis response does not guarantee a return to precrisis growth patterns in the face of weak recoveries in the major markets of the advanced countries. So the central unsettled question in 2009 was whether the emerging markets could sustain their growth in the context of a global economy that was being held back by the advanced economies. The answer now appears to be that they can. This is a new feature of the global economy. Ten years ago, the dependencies in terms of markets and aggregate demand would have been such that growth in the advanced economies was required to sustain the demand side of the growth in emerging markets. This has to do with composition as well as the size of emerging-market demand. It now appears that they have reached an aggregate size, a level of income (which shifts the composition of demand), and a pattern of direct intra-emerging-market trade that is capable of sustaining this growth.

However, decoupling is not an either/or matter. A major downturn in Europe or North America would subtract enough demand to slow growth in the emerging markets. Similarly, persistently high unemployment or low growth in advanced countries could cause a rise in protectionist measures, which if large enough would reduce external demand enough to affect trade and growth. Thus far, that has not happened. Finally, China's growth is a large and growing part of the emerging-market total, so China's ability to sustain growth through the middle-income transition, a stage of growth and development that it is entering, will be a third decisive factor. China is the largest trading partner on the export side for a growing list of countries, including Japan, Korea, India, and most of its smaller Asian neighbors. It is the largest trading partner (share of imports plus exports) for six of the Group of Twenty countries.

The rising systemic importance of the emerging markets has created new challenges. For China and prospectively for India, it has caused their global effects and responsibilities to expand at relatively low levels of per-capita income by historical standards. This is the direct result of sustained high growth over long periods of time in countries with populations approaching 20 percent of the world's population each. No one—these countries, their predecessors, or the global system as a whole—has figured out how to balance the complex requirements of sustaining growth and development domestically with the need to adapt to the changing environment to achieve stability in the system as a whole. It is clear that the balancing approach is the right one. A narrow focus on the domestic agenda is no longer feasible.

The implications are several. Much of the postwar global system involved a hybrid in which the advanced countries adopted policies that were designed to promote growth and keep the system stable. The developing countries had relatively little systemic impact on the system as a whole (because of small size) and therefore were free to focus on policies that promoted growth. With the increasing size of the latter, this convenient hybrid cannot continue to work. An example is the exchange-rate system, with floating market-determined rates for advanced countries and managed currencies and capital accounts in developing countries (in varying forms depending on size, state of development, and other factors). The challenge now is to build a new system that achieves goals of equity and fairness and stability but that also recognizes that open capital accounts and purely market-determined exchange rates probably entail too much risk for the systemically important emerging markets. A case in point is the expansion of interventions in capital flows in the postcrisis period to manage and limit the adverse effects of large capital inflows that stem in part from the accommodative monetary policies in advanced countries. From a longer-term perspective, emerging markets are a double-edged sword for the advanced countries. They lower the cost of many goods and represent growing external-market opportunities. But they also present challenges in terms of employment and scope in the tradable part of the advanced economies. And there are potential income-distribution effects that are hard to manage.

Since China is a key factor in global and emerging-market growth, it is worth devoting a few words to the challenges on that front. As noted above, China is entering the middle-income transition, a passage that has slowed many of its predecessors. The known high-speed middle-income transitions have thus far been confined to the economies of Japan, Korea, Taiwan Province of China, Singapore, and Hong Kong SAR.

At least five linked transitions are embedded in the next phase of China's growth, and they have been envisaged in the country's twelfth five-year plan:

- Change the country's growth model or supply-side structure as its labor costs rise, its global market shares get large enough to limit expansion, and advanced countries' growth momentum and tailwind decline for an unknown period of time;
- Rebalance demand from investment and exports to domestic consumption;
- Accommodate a rapidly urbanizing population, and structure incentives so that the process is as orderly as possible;
- Build the social infrastructure necessary for achieving a harmonious society with special emphasis on opportunity; and
- Take on international responsibilities for stability, growth, and sustainability (including tackling climate change) in a way that is commensurate with its growing size and systemic impact.

The challenge at this point is implementation. One needed set of reforms and system changes involves the allocation of capital in the government and state-owned enterprise sectors. Here a portion of the investment portfolio tends toward low private and social-return investments that seem to be driven more by the availability of funds than by returns. This is a deceptive trap. Such investment constitutes aggregate demand and supports growth in the short run but lacks the intertemporal multiplier effects of high-return investments. Eventually, the growth engine slows down. So the challenge will be to build the market and institutional mechanisms to redirect these funds to household income, higher-return investments, or important social services and social insurance systems.

I conclude this discussion of various aspects of growth in the global economy with a look at structural issues of a longer-term nature in the advanced economies. These are related indirectly to the current crisis in that the patterns of growth in the global economy preceding the crisis had the side effect of hiding some structural changes.

Some recent work on the changing structure of the U.S. economy can help begin to bring the issues into focus. Here I can only hint at the analysis. In the U.S. economy in the eighteen years immediately prior to the crisis, the economy produced a net increment of 27 million jobs. Virtually all (98 percent) of them were in the nontradable part of the economy, with the leading sectors in terms of size and increments being government, health care, retail, construction, and hotels, restaurants, and food service. On the tradable side, value added grew, but employment did not. Within the tradable sector, a number of high-value-added-per-employee service sectors—finance, computer design and engineering, management of enterprises, consulting—grew. The remainder, consisting of manufacturing sectors that have long and complex value-added chains, experienced value-added increases and employment declines. The net effect was rapidly rising value added per person in the tradable sector combined with negligible net employment growth.

It is fairly clear that the underlying trend is the movement offshore of a growing subset of the supply chains in U.S. manufacturing and some tradable services. Overlaid on top is a pattern of rapid technological advance, some of which is labor saving in nature. In some ways, in the face of these trends, it is remarkable that there was not an obvious employment problem.

The unbalanced and unsustainable pattern of growth leading up to the crisis, with excess consumption as a key component, appears to have allowed the nontradable sector to absorb most of the incremental labor force and delayed the arrival of market forces that would have caused a different pattern of structural change. There is at least a question about whether precrisis employment patterns will continue in the postcrisis period. One view is that this is a long, difficult recovery by historical standards but not much more than that. I believe that the United States cannot return to the precrisis mixture of aggregate demand with zero household savings and that the lost aggregate demand will have to be replaced by investment and foreign demand. The latter implies an expansion in the tradable sector and probably an expansion in the scope of the tradable sector.

In addition, restoring competitiveness in an expanded part of the tradable sector may have consequences for incomes and the income distribution. The precrisis trends in income distribution certainly included relatively rapid increases in incomes at the upper end of the spectrum and low to flat incomes in the midrange.

Much more remains to be done on this front, including a detailed assessment of the structural shifts in other advanced economies, which are presumably subject to similar global market forces but which appear to respond in different ways, generating different outcomes in terms of structure, employment, and income distribution.

We were going to get to this stage in the global economy, with or without a crisis. Perhaps the crisis has brought the structural and distributional issues into focus more quickly. For several decades, the distributional effects of the evolution of the postwar global economy were largely benign, with a successful postwar recovery in the advanced countries followed by 2.5 percent real growth and little serious unemployment. In parallel, the developing economies with varying starting points engaged with the global economy, found avenues for inbound knowledge transfer and a large advanced-country demand, and accelerated to previously unknown sustained high growth rates. After several decades of this pattern, the developing economies are larger and richer. Given the way that market forces and growth dynamics work, it seems likely that we are entering a more challenging period from the standpoint of distributional issues and that it is relatively uncharted territory.

Looking forward, the major new policy challenges related to growth, both domestically and internationally, seem to fall into two categories—sustainability and distribution. There is no particular reason to think that institutional and policy adaptation combined with human ingenuity will prove inadequate to the task. But it will take time to bring these evolving new issues into focus, a prerequisite for dealing with them.

VI

The International Monetary System

Questions: How Should the Crisis Affect Our Views of the International Monetary System?

The early phase of the global economic crisis that began in 2008 was dominated by large capital outflows, induced foreign-liquidity shortages, and, in some cases, large induced changes in exchange rates. The current phase is characterized by large capital inflows, strong appreciation pressure on many currencies, concern about currency manipulation, and talk of currency wars. So it is not surprising that the French have put reform of the international monetary system at the top of their agenda for the Group of Twenty presidency.

Reform of the international monetary system means many things to many people, from increases in allocations of special drawing rights (SDRs) to the creation of a global currency. But it includes at least the following issues (some of which overlap with issues of capital-account management).

Global Liquidity Provision

When the crisis started, some investors looked for safe havens, others needed to repatriate funds, and many countries faced large capital outflows. These actions led to funding problems and, in some cases, to sharp depreciations and adverse balance-sheet effects. These effects were attenuated in some countries through the use of previously accumulated reserves (although on a surprisingly limited scale), and in others through the provision of swap lines from foreign central banks. Later, these swap lines were supplemented by the provision of liquidity through new International Monetary Fund (IMF) windows, first the flexible credit line and more recently the precautionary credit line.

The main question is whether the current arrangements can be improved. Precautionary saving in the form of reserve accumulation is socially inefficient. Bilateral swap lines benefit some countries but not others. Various arrangements have been proposed. Some have suggested increasing allocations of SDRs, although allocation rules would have to be seriously modified before the allocations could go to the countries most likely to need them. The IMF has explored extensions of the flexible credit line and the creation of a global stabilization mechanism, a contingent liquidity window that would provide liquidity to a large number of countries but only under conditions of high systemic risk. Others have suggested that swap lines be run through the IMF rather than bilaterally.

In all these cases, the central issue is conditionality, and whether the degree of conditionality should be a function of the state of the world economy. In times of high systemic risk, conditions should probably be less stringent than in normal times. Another issue is the degree to which the development of such liquidity provision would affect the accumulation of reserves by emerging-market countries.

Current-Account Balances

The crisis and adjustments following the peak of the crisis have led to a reexamination of current-account imbalances. The issue is whether countries, right or wrong, should be free to run large current-account imbalances or whether there should be multilateral rules of the game.

Some have argued that large current-account deficits may be dangerous not only for the countries running them but for others as well—an argument similar to the effects of actions by large financial institutions on systemic risk. Others have argued that in the current context, large current-account surpluses are impeding the world recovery. Given that many advanced countries cannot increase domestic demand, they need to increase net exports. For this to happen, the other countries, at least those that can increase their domestic demand, should correspondingly decrease their net exports.

Should there be rules governing current-account balances (as suggested by the U.S. Treasury)? Are current-account balances the right variable, or at least the least bad variable, to focus on? Can realistic rules be designed? Can they be enforced? These questions are related to issues raised in discussions of capital-account management. Should there be rules on reserve accumulation and on capital controls? If so, how can they be enforced?

Reserve Currencies

Another old issue is that of the dominance of the dollar as a reserve currency. The fact that both central banks and private investors see U.S. Treasury bills as a safe asset has allowed the United States to finance its current-account deficit easily; some have called this, somewhat misleadingly, an exorbitant privilege. During the acute phases of the current crisis, it led to strong capital inflows into the United States and dollar appreciation.

Some have argued that this exorbitant privilege should end and that the world should have multiple reserve currencies. Is it desirable? Is it feasible? Currencies do not become reserve currencies by fiat or privilege. Investors want to hold U.S. Treasury bills because the Treasury bill market is deep and liquid. Thus, the question is whether other markets, such as the market for euro bonds, can offer similar advantages.

Some have argued that the special drawing rights could become a reserve currency. This would require the creation of a deep and liquid market in SDR-denominated bonds. The same questions as above arise. Would it be desirable? Is it feasible? Is there enough demand and supply for such bonds to create a deep and liquid market? Could, for example, the IMF, which lends in SDRs, create some of the supply by partly financing itself through the issuance of SDR bonds?

These questions do not exhaust the list. Old questions such as fixed-versus floating-rate arrangements and the existence of optimal currency areas must also be revisited. One interesting aspect of the crisis is that countries with fixed exchange rates do not appear to have done systematically worse than those with floating rates. The difficulties faced by a number of euro members in adjusting to idiosyncratic shocks also require a reconsideration of the costs and benefits of common currency areas.

20

The Implications of Cross-Border Banking and Foreign-Currency Swap Lines for the International Monetary System

Már Guðmundsson

The financial crisis in Iceland that struck with full force in 2008 throws light on one of the more important fault lines at the intersection between the international monetary system and the international financial system.[1] This fault line was the operation of cross-border banks with large foreign-currency balance sheets featuring significant maturity mismatches but without an effective lender of last resort (LOLR) in terms of foreign currency.[2]

In this chapter, I concentrate mostly on this fault line, its implications for the international monetary system, and potential remedies, leaving aside many other important issues regarding the international monetary system.[3] This topic leads to other key issues, such as the reserve currency, a global lender of last resort, and the role of foreign-exchange reserves.

My former colleagues at the Bank for International Settlements (BIS) and others have described in several articles and reports how foreign-exchange risk in cross-border banking (currency mismatches and maturity mismatches in foreign currency) accumulated prior to the crisis, how that risk materialized in a forceful way after the collapse of Lehman Brothers, and how the ensuing dollar shortage was prevented from triggering widespread failure of banks to deliver on their foreign-currency payments by lender-of-last-resort operations in foreign exchange, using countries' reserves and the dollar swap lines that were granted on a large scale.[4] The same episode played out in the case of the Icelandic banks but with a less happy ending, although there was much more to that story that I cannot expand on here, such as hidden vulnerabilities in the capital positions of the banks.

Maturity mismatches are the bread and butter of modern banking, although they make banks vulnerable to runs. In the case of solvent institutions, we have known theoretically since Henry Thornton (1802) (and probably over a century, as a practical policy) how to deal with that vulnerability in a domestic setting—with central bank LOLR operations, later complemented by deposit insurance. This process is facilitated by two factors. First, the funds withdrawn from banks during a domestic run flow in one form or another to the central bank, which can then redirect them back to the banks. Second, central banks have a very large short-run capacity to expand their balance sheets.

In the current setting, it is far from guaranteed that this process can be replicated at the international level. In normal times, managing liquidity across currencies from countries with free movement of capital and relatively developed capital markets is not much of an issue. In these conditions, foreign-exchange swap markets can speedily be used to convert liquidity from one currency to another at spreads that closely reflect the differences in domestic money-market rates in the two countries concerned. In other words, the covered-interest parity condition broadly holds. But runs are less likely in normal times. During the peak of the crisis, this process broke down almost completely in many cases, and foreign-exchange swap spreads skyrocketed afterward. It became extremely costly and in some cases almost impossible to convert domestic liquidity into dollar liquidity. The same scenario played out with the euro for several European countries outside the euro area.

In a situation like this, the home central bank's ability to help banks refinance the foreign liquidity that was denied them on the market is limited by the size of its reserves or the willingness of its larger neighbors to help. The Icelandic case brought this into sharp relief. Just before their failure, the three cross-border banks had foreign-currency balance sheets amounting to almost seven and a half times gross domestic product. In comparison, the reserves of the Central Bank of Iceland, including swap lines with Nordic countries and committed credit lines, amounted to around 35 percent of GDP. Even if some of the foreign-currency liabilities were long-term, the reserves were no match for the bleeding balance sheets of the banks.

The issue here is one of the ebb and flow of international liquidity, which is a monetary issue. Although the provision of foreign-currency liquidity through reserves was important during the crisis, most studies seem to support the conclusion that the dollar swap lines made the key difference, especially when they were uncapped for some key central banks. It was to a significant degree the domestic LOLR process replicated at the international level.

Does this mean that we have the solution? At the conceptual level, yes, but at the practical level, no. The swap lines are not a permanent and reliable feature of the international monetary system. Will they be resurrected if similar circumstances arise in the future? Excellent central-bank cooperation and strong leadership were involved on this occasion. However, we have seen their existence challenged in political discussion in the United States. Although at this time it was dollar liquidity that was needed around the globe, next time it might be other currencies. And then there is the issue of access criteria. Who gets a swap line and who does not? Should the provision of international liquidity be subject to the decision of one national central bank? It is also possible to turn the question around and ask whether it would ever work for an international process to decide on a major expansion of the balance sheet of a national central bank. After all, the foreign-exchange swaps amounted to over a quarter of the balance sheet of the Federal Reserve at the peak (Moessner and Allen 2010a), and then there was the promise of an uncapped expansion for a few key central banks.

What are the alternatives? One is to change the international financial system as a result of the problems revealed in the international monetary system. This requires the contraction of cross-border banking through market processes, including subsidiarization and local funding. Countries need to adopt measures to deal with risks by restricting the international activities of home banks and placing stricter prudential limits on currency mismatches and foreign-currency maturity mismatches. For example, when Iceland lifts its current capital controls on outflows, it probably will impose restrictions on both the size and composition of the foreign-currency balance sheets of home-headquartered banks. Some might see such restrictions as capital controls in another form, but I see them as prudential rules.

These developments might restrict significant cross-border banking to larger countries with international currencies, but this need not be all bad. The structure of cross-border banking would then be adjusting to the real risks involved, but I suspect that some smaller countries might not like it. In Europe, smaller countries have the option of joining the European Union and the euro area, which makes it safer to be a home base to cross-border banks. EU-wide (or European Monetary Union-wide) supervision, deposit insurance, and crisis management and resolution were put in place for such banks in the future. This might even entail two types of bank licenses—one for domestic banks and another for those wanting to have substantial operations across borders.

Increased self-insurance by countries building foreign-exchange reserves is also an alternative, and this has happened after the crisis.[5] However, there are well-known drawbacks and limitations to this option.

Another currently discussed alternative is to strengthen the IMF as an international lender of last resort and, in the process, enhance the role of the special drawing rights (SDRs) as a reserve asset. It would involve making the supply of SDRs more elastic and the process more conducive to managing international liquidity. In the grander visions, the SDR would run parallel to the U.S. dollar as a reserve currency and potentially replace it.[6] Such an arrangement would be a move in the direction of John Keynes's (1980) original idea of an international clearing union and its currency, the Bancor. This idea merits further research and full discussion, and I note that the IMF is doing substantial work in this area. At this point, however, I see several obstacles.

First, there is a distinction between lending to sovereigns and lending to banks. The IMF has focused on lending to sovereigns, whereas swap lines were actually a form of lending to banks because, from a liquidity standpoint, the foreign central banks were simply intermediaries of the Federal Reserve's global liquidity operations, although the counterparty risk was borne by the foreign central banks. In the initial stages of a financial crisis, banks can encounter foreign-currency liquidity problems even if the finances of the sovereign are in good shape and there is no balance-of-payments crisis. Even solid Norway struggled on this point for a few days post-Lehman Brothers. The central bank was able to manage with its own reserves, but to be on the safe side and probably to contain the liquidation of U.S. dollar assets, a swap arrangement was swiftly negotiated with the Federal Reserve, at the same time that the Fed made comparable agreements with several other central banks. However, as was seen in several cases during this last episode, a banking crisis in a small, open economy will affect the sovereign in due course and may ultimately result in a full-scale fiscal crisis.

Second, the special drawing right itself is not at present a currency in its own right but a claim to use other members' currencies or foreign-exchange reserves. For the SDR to become a truly international currency on a par with the U.S. dollar, it needs robust payment and settlement systems, and the private sector will have to be induced to use it on a large scale. In addition, if alterations in the supply of special drawing rights are going to be an important tool for managing international liquidity, not to mention using it for lender-of-last-resort operations for international banks, then the IMF needs to be able to create liquidity or swiftly tap into those that can. Furthermore, speed and scale are of the essence if such an option is to be a viable alternative to the swap lines.

Third, the governance mechanisms for such a new global reserve currency do not exist. It is hard to envision the current IMF executive board taking decisions that are more akin to what central banks do, such as setting special drawing right interest rates (if and when it gets a life of its own) or acting quickly to decide on lender-of-last-resort operations that are basically directed at banks, although probably through national central banks. What is needed is possibly some kind of International Liquidity Committee composed of central-bank governors and perhaps full-time executive directors. Maybe it should meet at the Bank for International Settlements. The arguments for central-bank independence that apply to monetary policy seem to carry over to affecting global monetary conditions.

In conclusion, the expansion of cross-border banking that was witnessed before the crisis was part of the ongoing and at least partly beneficial process of financial globalization. However, if we do not deal with the risks involved, we face the danger of a major reversal. It is fine to elaborate on grand schemes, and one day they might be realized. In the meantime, we can expect a combination of a partial retreat of cross-border banking, increased self-insurance, expansion of regional arrangements, and partial reforms to the international monetary and financial systems. Speedier and more flexible credit lines at the IMF are certainly a welcome part of the latter. Let us hope that the reforms will dominate the retreat.

Notes

1. There are many definitions of the terms *international monetary system* and *international financial system* and their relationship to each other. I construe the former to consist of exchange-rate arrangements, payments and settlement systems across borders, and other international factors that would be included in the definition of a domestic monetary system (including liquidity provision by a lender of last resort), and the institutions and the rules that apply to all of these. The international financial system consists of the operations of financial institutions and markets across borders as shaped by market forces and domestic and international regulations. In some sense, capital flows belong to both, as they go through markets and institutions but are conditioned by factors such as exchange-rate regimes and exchange-rate restrictions.

2. See Guðmundsson and Thorgeirsson (2010). On the financial crisis in Iceland more generally, see Guðmundsson (2010) and references therein, and "Report of the Special Investigation Commission (SIC)," http://sic.althingi.is.

3. Bernanke (2011) and Carney (2010) provide interesting recent analysis of one of the important omitted issues—the functioning of the adjustment mechanism.

4. See, for instance, Baba and Shim (2010); CGFS Study Group (2010a, 2010b, 2010c); Fender and McGuire (2010a, 2010b); McGuire and von Peter (2009); Moessner and Allen (2010 a, 2010b); and Obstfeld (2010). For the Korean case, see Park (2010).

5. Moessner and Allen (2010a) report sizable increases in reserves in the case of Denmark, Sweden, Hungary, and Brazil.

6. On a much-discussed proposal, see Zhou (2009). The International Monetary Fund (2011) provides an interesting analysis of the issues involved.

References

Baba, Naohiko, and Ilhyock Shim. 2010. "Policy Responses to Dislocations in the FX Swap Market: The Experience of Korea." *BIS Quarterly Review* (June), http://www.bis.org.

Bernanke, Ben S. 2011. "Global Imbalances: Links to Economic and Financial Stability." Paper presented at the Banque de France Financial Stability Review Launch Event, Paris, France, February 18, http://www.bis.org.

Carney, Mark. 2010. "Restoring Faith in the International Monetary System." Paper presented at the Spruce Meadows Changing Fortunes Round Table, Calgary, Alberta, September 10, http://www.bis.org.

Committee on the Global Financial System (CGFS) Study Group. 2010a. "The Functioning and Resilience of Cross-border Funding Markets." CGFS Paper No. 37 (March), http://www.bis.org.

Committee on the Global Financial System (CGFS) Study Group. 2010b. "Funding Patterns and Liquidity Management of Internationally Active Banks." CGFS Paper No. 39 (May), http://www.bis.org.

Committee on the Global Financial System (CGFS) Study Group. 2010c. "Long-term Issues in International Banking." CGFS Paper No. 41 (July), http://www .bis.org.

Fender, Ingo, and Patrick McGuire. 2010a. "Bank Structure, Funding Risk and the Transmission of Shocks across Countries: Concepts and Measurement." *BIS Quarterly Review* (September), http://www.bis.org.

Fender, Ingo, and Patrick McGuire. 2010b. "European Banks' U.S. Dollar Funding Pressures." *BIS Quarterly Review* (June), http://www.bis.org.

Guðmundsson, Már. 2010. "The Financial Crisis in Iceland and the Fault Lines in Cross-Border Banking." Paper presented at the FIBE (Fagkonferanse I Bedrift-søkonomiske Emner) conference, Bergen, Norway, January 7, http://www. sedlabanki.is/?PageID=287&NewsID=2362.

Guðmundsson, Már, and Thorsteinn Thorgeirsson. 2010. "The Fault Lines in Cross-Border Banking: Lessons from the Icelandic Case." SUERF Studies 05/2010, European Money and Finance Forum, http://www.suerf.org/download/studies/study20105.pdf.

International Monetary Fund (IMF). 2011. "Enhancing International Monetary Stability: A Role for the SDR?" International Monetary Fund Paper, International Monetary Fund, Washington, DC, January 7.

Keynes, John Maynard. 1980. *The Collected Writings of John Maynard Keynes.* Vol. 25, *Activities 1940–1944. Shaping the Post-War World: The Clearing Union.* Edited by Donald Moggridge. London: Macmillan Cambridge University Press.

McGuire, Patrick, and Götz von Peter. 2009. "The U.S. Dollar Shortage in Global Banking and the International Policy Response." Bank of International Settlements Working Paper No. 291 (October), http://www.bis.org.

Moessner, Richhild, and William A. Allen. 2010a. "Banking Crises and the International Monetary System in the Great Depression and Now." Bank of International Settlements Working Paper No. 333 (December), http://www.bis.org.

Moessner, Richhild, and William A. Allen. 2010b. "Options for Meeting the Demand for International Liquidity during Financial Crises." *BIS Quarterly Review* (September), http://www.bis.org.

Obstfeld, Maurice. 2010. "Expanding Gross Asset Positions and the International Monetary System." Paper presented at the Federal Reserve Bank of Kansas City symposium, Macroeconomic Challenges: The Decade Ahead, Jackson Hole, Wyoming, August 26–28.

Park, Yung Chul. 2010. "The Role of Macroprudential Policy for Financial Stability in East Asia's Emerging Economies." Korea University, September.

Thornton, Henry. 1802. *An Enquiry into the Nature and Effects of the Paper Credit of Great Britain.* London: George Allen & Unwin.

Zhou, Xiaochuan. 2009. "Reform the International Monetary System." *BIS Review* 41/2009 (March 23), http://www.bis.org.

21

The International Monetary System

Olivier Jeanne

This chapter about the international monetary system is structured around two themes—global financial imbalances and global financial safety nets.

Global Imbalances and Global Safety Nets

Many economists think that improving global financial safety nets will help address the problem of global imbalances. The idea is that global imbalances come in part from the accumulation of reserves by emerging-market countries trying to self-insure against volatile capital flows. Thus, better safety nets, in addition to their intrinsic merits, will reduce the need for self-insurance through precautionary savings and will mitigate the global savings glut.

How important for global imbalances is the precautionary accumulation of reserves? One answer is given in figure 21.1. This figure reports the current-account surplus of all the countries that had a surplus in 2003 to 2005 according to the World Economic Outlook database, excluding oil-exporting countries. (The oil exporters have been removed because they accumulate foreign assets for reasons that are specific to those countries and that we understand pretty well.) The data cover 2000 to 2015, so the last third of the graph is based on a forecast by the International Monetary Fund.

In this group, the "sudden stop" countries either had a sudden stop between 1995 and 2000 or benefited from a swap with the U.S. Federal Reserve or other central banks in 2008.[1] These countries can be thought of as the natural customers of the global financial safety nets. The figure shows, in black, the share of the surplus that comes from those countries.

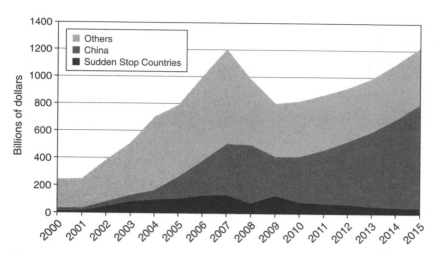

Figure 21.1
Current account balances of surplus countries. *Source:* World Economic Outlook (2010).

It also shows the contribution of China (in dark gray) and the rest (including Germany and Japan).

Figure 21.1 highlights two striking facts. First, the self-insurance motive accounts for a small and decreasing share of the current-account imbalances. Thus, improving global financial safety nets is important but should not be expected to reduce global imbalances significantly. The second striking fact is the size of China's contribution to global surpluses, especially looking forward. The World Economic Outlook (WEO) predicts that China will account for more than 60 percent of the global surplus (excluding oil exporters). So if there is one topic to focus on for understanding global imbalances, it is China.

The Chinese Dilemma

In this chapter, I develop the thesis that the capital-account policies of China are key to understanding why the Chinese current-account surplus is very large. My analysis is based on a model I presented in a recent paper (Jeanne 2011), but this simple model is consistent with what many people think China is doing.

To understand how the model works, think of an open economy in which the government uses two policy instruments. First, the government uses capital controls to determine the volume of gross capital inflows, and second, the public sector of this economy accumulates a large stock of foreign assets. It stands to reason—and the model shows—that by playing with these two instruments, the country can control the level of net foreign assets for the country as a whole. Essentially, the controls on capital inflows prevent the accumulation of foreign assets by the public sector from being offset by capital inflows to the private sector.

This simple point has important implications. If the government controls the country's net foreign assets, it controls the current-account balance, which is the change in net foreign assets. From there, it is easy to see that it also controls the trade balance and that the real exchange rate must be at the level that is consistent with the trade balance. The causality goes from the trade balance to the real exchange rate rather than from the real exchange rate to the trade balance.

This is not a completely conventional way of presenting Chinese policies because it does not involve the monetary authorities in an essential way. The more conventional view is that the Chinese central bank resists the nominal appreciation of the renminbi through foreign-exchange interventions. The conventional view, however, misses an important point: if the Chinese authorities only buy reserves, then they could resist only the nominal appreciation of the renminbi, not the real appreciation, which would still come about through domestic inflation.

Controls on capital inflows come into play by preventing the internal appreciation of the renminbi by repressing domestic demand. Those controls make it possible to maintain a sustained real undervaluation of the renminbi. But when capital controls are introduced into the model, it is possible to abstract from monetary policy and build a model in which the real exchange rate is determined entirely by capital-account policies. The central bank's foreign-exchange interventions are the way that the Chinese public sector accumulates foreign assets in practice. But this is not essential: the foreign assets could be accumulated through a different channel at the margin without impairing the authorities from undervaluing the real exchange rate. Capital-account policies, in this view, are the linchpin of China's exchange-rate policy.

If this view is correct, it has several implications. First, consider the vexing question of how to reduce the Chinese saving rate. My hypothesis is that the Chinese authorities induce a form of forced saving in China through their capital-account policies. One way of understanding this is that at the same time that the Chinese public sector is purchasing large volumes of foreign assets, it also is forcing the domestic private sector to buy large volumes of yuan-denominated assets (sterilization bonds and bank deposits) that cannot be sold to foreign investors because of the capital controls. The domestic income that is spent on those assets cannot be spent on consumption; it is a form of forced saving.

There are other explanations for the high Chinese saving rate, as well, including the lack of social insurance, aging, and financial underdevelopment.[2] But if you believe these other explanations, then you have to believe that not much would happen if China relaxed its controls on capital inflows because the Chinese government is holding the stock of net foreign assets that the Chinese private sector wants to hold. If you think that relaxing the controls on inflows would lead to more inflows on a net basis, then you must believe in some version of the model that I have outlined.

Which explanation you believe has important implications for the structural reforms that would be required to increase Chinese demand. Based on the other explanations for high saving mentioned above, the required reforms should be to "increase social insurance, strengthen corporate governance, and implement reforms to increase access to credit for households and SMEs in China."[3] However, if the high Chinese saving rate is due primarily to its capital-account policies, then those structural reforms are unlikely to increase Chinese demand much. Instead, the focus should be on the capital-account policies of China and, more precisely, on giving foreign investors a larger access to Chinese financial and monetary assets.

The Chinese capital-account policies are closely related to the internationalization of the renminbi. There are important debates (which I do not have space to discuss here) about the transition from a dollar-based international monetary system to a multipolar world with three or four reserve currencies, perhaps including the renminbi (Eichengreen 2011). The Chinese authorities seem to have adopted the objective of internationalizing the renminbi, although the pace and the modalities of the transition are not clear. However, making a reserve currency of the renminbi would require giving foreign investors access to a substantial stock of yuan-dominated financial assets. That is, it would mean relaxing the controls on capital inflows and losing control over the real exchange rate.

The transition from a strictly controlled capital account to a less controlled one is fraught with difficulties. The concerns of the Chinese authorities, as I understand them, are twofold. The first concern is about the pace of this transition—to preserve the benefits of an undervalued renminbi in terms of export-led growth until an alternative engine of growth is up and running. The second concern is about the orderliness of the transition—to avoid a scenario with speculative inflows overflowing the capital-account barriers and leading to an abrupt appreciation of the renminbi, which could be very disruptive for the Chinese economy.

Those concerns are both understandable and legitimate, but there is a tension between the two. On the one hand, the Chinese authorities might want to err on the side of caution and implement a slow transition ("crossing the river by feeling the stones"). On the other hand, the slower the transition, the more foreign assets will be accumulated, the more pressure will build up, and the more difficult it will be to achieve an orderly exit. Therefore, an orderly exit strategy requires a measured—but not too measured—pace. How the Chinese authorities will resolve this dilemma is key for the future shape of the international monetary system.

The Rules of the Game for International Capital Flows

Should China be treated sui generis, or should it be included in a wider concept of the rules of the game for the global economic system? I would argue in favor of the latter—more precisely, that it makes sense to put the case of China in the context of a multilateral framework for the management of capital flows.

The status quo is characterized by an indefensible asymmetry between strong international rules for trade in goods (with the World Trade Organization) and a quasi-absence of international rules for international trade in assets. This asymmetry is indefensible because (as I show in Jeanne 2011) any country can use capital-account restrictions to manipulate its real exchange rate in a way that reproduces the effects of a combination of tariff and subsidy. What sense does it make to discourage trade distortions while putting no restriction on capital-account policies?

This does not mean that all capital controls are bad. There is a strong case for emerging-market economies to use prudential controls to deal with booms and busts in capital flows.[4] There have been calls for developing a code of good practices with regard to prudential capital controls that would increase the predictability and reduce the stigma associated with the use of such policies. And the International Monetary Fund has been asked by its shareholders to look into the question of whether there is a need for globally agreed-on rules of the road for the management of capital flows (Strauss-Kahn 2011).

If one is going to develop a code of good practice for prudential controls on capital flows, it would make sense to take an additional step forward and also think about using the code to define, by exclusion, the capital controls that cannot be justified on prudential grounds, are presumably distortive, and should be relaxed (Jeanne, Subramanian, and Williamson 2011).

There are several advantages from focusing the multilateral discussion on capital-account policies. The discussion would be focused on the policy instruments rather than on the outcomes. As I understand it, the multilateral assessment program conducted by the Group of Twenty to reduce global imbalances relies on targets (or indicators) for outcome variables such as current-account balances. This is problematic because economic theory does not give us models that we trust enough to determine the appropriate (undistorted) levels of variables such as current-account balances or the policy instruments that should be used to achieve targets for such variables. This also applies to real exchange rates. A more direct approach that focuses on policy instruments seems preferable.

To sum up, there might be considerable (although not immediate) benefits from trying to agree on rules of the game that recognize the link between free trade in goods and a certain degree of freedom in trade in assets—that full participation in the world trading system should be premised on a certain degree of freedom in trade in assets.

Global Financial Safety Nets

The motivation for reforming global financial safety nets is well known. Emerging-market countries did not rely on the existing multilateral

Table 21.1
International reserves

Country	Korea	Brazil	Singapore	Mexico
Reserves September 2008	$240 billion	$206 billion	$169 billion	$99 billion
Federal Reserve swap	30 billion	30 billion	30 billion	30 billion

arrangements (such as the IMF or the Chiang Mai Initiative) to obtain international liquidity in the fall of 2008 and relied instead on swaps with the U.S. Federal Reserve and other central banks. The question is how the multilateral arrangements for international liquidity provision can be improved. This question is largely orthogonal to global imbalances (as I argued above), but it is nonetheless important for emerging-market countries and has received a lot of attention under the Korean chairmanship of the G20.

The answer to one question—why did the swaps make a difference?—really matters for how we design global financial safety nets. As shown in table 21.1, the four emerging-market economies that received swaps from the U.S. Federal Reserve—Korea, Brazil, Singapore, and Mexico—already had reserves that were a multiple of those swaps. For example, Korea had more than $200 billion in reserves when it received a $30 billion swap. Why would a $30 billion swap make a difference for a country that has $240 billion in reserves?

I can think of four hypotheses, which are listed below:

- *Psychological threshold* The swaps made it possible to maintain the headline level of reserves above a psychological threshold. For example, there were reports that the Korean authorities believed that reserves should be maintained above $200 billion to maintain market confidence.

- *Seal of approval* The Fed signaled that it had a positive view of the prospects for the Korean economy, which in turn improved market expectations.

- *Lender-of-last-resort* The Fed, as the true lender of last resort for dollars (the creator of the currency), was implicitly committing itself to lend further if necessary. The difference from the previous explanation is that the signal was about the Fed rather than about Korea.

• *Minor part of a policy package*   The swaps did not really matter. They were components of a larger set of policies that restored a measure of confidence at the center (Wall Street).

It is difficult to distinguish empirically between these views, but I believe more in the final two explanations than in the first two. That is, the Fed swaps mattered more than the $30 billion that was provided to Korea because the Fed is a true lender of last resort and because the support to Korea was part of a larger package that restored a measure of confidence at the center. If this is correct, then the fact that the resources were provided by a central bank—the creator of the currency—was essential to why the swaps had a positive effect. That would mean that for the global financial safety nets to be as effective as possible, they should involve central banks and institutionalize the swaps in some way.[5] If it is politically unfeasible for the major central banks to make such commitments, emerging-market countries will have to rely more on prudential capital controls to reduce their exposure to capital-flow volatility.

Notes

1. A *sudden stop* is defined as a fall in the financial account of more than 5 percent of gross domestic product. The list of sudden stops comes from Jeanne and Rancière (2011). The list of countries that benefited from swaps can be found in Aizenman, Jinjarak, and Park (2010, table 2).

2. For the lack of social insurance, see Chamon and Prasad (2010). For financial underdevelopment, see Caballero, Farhi, and Gourinchas (2008) or Song, Storesletten, and Zilibotti (2011).

3. The quote is from Blanchard and Milesi-Ferretti (2009).

4. For more details, see Jeanne and Korinek (2010) and Jeanne, Subramanian, and Williamson (2011).

5. This could be done through the International Monetary Fund, as proposed by Truman (2008).

References

Aizenman, Joshua, Yothin Jinjarak, and Donghyun Park. 2010. "International Reserves and Swap Lines: Substitutes or Complements?" Manuscript. http://economics.ucsc.edu/research/downloads/AJP-IR-SW-2010-July.pdfSOURCE.

Blanchard, Olivier, and Gian Maria Milesi-Ferretti. 2009. "Global Imbalances: In Midstream?" International Monetary Fund Staff Position Note 09/29, International Monetary Fund, Washington, DC.

Caballero, Ricardo, Emmanuel Farhi, and Pierre-Olivier Gourinchas. 2008. "An Equilibrium Model of 'Global Imbalances' and Low Interest Rates." *American Economic Review* 98 (1):358–393.

Chamon, Marcos, and Eswar Prasad. 2010. "Why Are the Savings Rates of Urban Households in China Rising?" *American Economic Journal: Macroeconomics* 2 (1):93–130.

Eichengreen, Barry. 2011. *Exorbitant Privilege: The Rise and Fall of the Dollar and the Future of the International Monetary System.* Oxford: Oxford University Press.

Jeanne, Olivier. 2011. "Capital Account Policies and the Real Exchange Rate." Department of Economics, Johns Hopkins University, Baltimore, MD.

Jeanne, Olivier, and Anton Korinek. 2010. "Excessive Volatility in Capital Flows: A Pigouvian Taxation Approach." *American Economic Review* 100:403–407.

Jeanne, Olivier, and Romain Rancière. 2011. "The Optimal Level of International Reserves for Emerging Market Countries: A New Formula and Some Applications." *Economic Journal* 121 (555):905–930.

Jeanne, Olivier, Arvind Subramanian, and John Williamson. 2011. *Who Needs to Open the Capital Account?* Washington, DC: Peterson Institute for International Economics.

Song, Zheng, Kjetil Storesletten, and Fabrizio Zilibotti. 2011. "Growing Like China." *American Economic Review* 101 (1):196–233.

Strauss-Kahn, Dominique. 2011. "Toward a More Stable International Monetary System." Opening remarks presented at the lecture and discussion, "Towards a More Stable International Monetary System." Washington, DC, February 10.

Truman, Edward. 2008. "On What Terms Is the IMF Worth Funding?" Peterson Institute Working Paper 08-11, Peterson Institute for International Economics, Washington, DC.

World Economic Outlook (WEO). 2010. International Monetary Fund, October.

22

International Monetary System Reform: A Practical Agenda

Charles Collyns

Reform of the international monetary system is always an intellectually stimulating topic, but sometimes it gets lost in abstruse debates that lead nowhere. The turbulent economic developments of the past several years underline that now is a moment when our collective attention needs to focus on a pragmatic policy agenda with real practical consequences.

In this chapter, I address three immediately relevant issues: first, ensuring effective international economic cooperation to achieve a sustained, well-balanced global recovery; second, moving to more consistently flexible exchange-rate management across all the major economies to support rebalancing and reduce the long-prevailing asymmetric bias in the international monetary system; and third, developing a consensus around a coherent framework for emerging economies to manage capital-flow volatility. I conclude by emphasizing the crucial role that the International Monetary Fund (IMF or the Fund) can play to advance this reform agenda by delivering more forceful surveillance.

International economic cooperation proved highly effective in dealing with the aftermath of the 2008 global financial crisis, when all Group of Twenty (G20) economies faced similar problems of grappling with a collapse in demand and confidence. The task now is harder but no less relevant. Recent global growth has been fragile and uneven. Much of the emerging world has grown rapidly but has faced risks of overheating. By contrast, in advanced economies, the recovery has been more gradual and recently has lost steam, output gaps and high unemployment remain serious concerns, and sustained fiscal consolidation will be needed over the medium term. This fragile and uneven recovery raises the specter that external imbalances could again widen, which could destabilize financial markets and threaten a period of weak global economic performance.

At the Pittsburgh Summit in September 2009, the G20 created the Framework for Strong, Sustainable, and Balanced Growth as a central foundation for effective cooperation across the world's largest economies.[1] We need to build on this framework to achieve consensus on joint efforts to identify the root causes of imbalances and agree on policies to address them. Success is imperative for the health of the global recovery and for the G20's credibility.

In Paris in February 2011, the G20 finance ministers agreed on a set of indicators to focus on large imbalances requiring policy action.[2] In Washington in April 2011, we agreed on indicative guidelines, and selected seven countries for more intensive study of the root causes of imbalances.[3] The next stage is to develop a concrete action plan and policy deliverables by leaders at the Cannes Summit in November 2011.

Successful rebalancing will require complementary actions across countries. Advanced countries, including the United States, will need to deliver credible multiyear reforms to restore fiscal sustainability. Other nations must play their part by undertaking the difficult reforms required to develop new sources of growth. Most important, major emerging economies with persistent current-account surpluses need to reduce their reliance on export-led growth and shift their economies toward domestic consumption and investment. This will require policy reforms to encourage robust growth of domestic demand and a corresponding shift in the pattern of supply toward domestic markets.

My second theme is the importance of persuading all major economies to allow exchange rates to move flexibly. The current international monetary system is an uneasy hybrid of flexible and heavily managed exchange rates. It is increasingly ill-suited to facilitating global adjustment as rapidly growing emerging economies with heavily managed exchange rates take on rising importance in the global economy. This is a new form of a long-standing asymmetry in the system, by which surplus countries do not face adequate pressure to let their currencies adjust.

The limited degree of currency flexibility in the world's largest exporter and second-largest economy, China, is of particular concern. China's currency remains substantially undervalued, notwithstanding some increased flexibility toward the dollar since June 2010. To avoid losing competitiveness relative to China, many of China's neighbors also intervene heavily and also have undervalued currencies. Such policies undermine the key role of the exchange rate in shifting the pattern of global supply and demand, imposing an undue burden on others and threatening to impede strong and sustainable global growth. All major economies, whether emerging or advanced, should be prepared to allow exchange rates to move to facilitate external adjustment in response to market forces.

My third and final topic is the need for consensus around a coherent policy framework for emerging economies to manage volatile capital flows. To some degree, this issue is receiving increased attention as a consequence of the previous two issues. A world with a multispeed recovery combining flexible and heavily managed currencies is one in which capital flows tend to be volatile, putting pressure on macroeconomic frameworks and threatening to exacerbate financial vulnerabilities.

Capital flows to emerging markets typically reflect strong growth and attractive rates of return and have the potential to help fill substantial investment needs. Particularly in countries with undervalued currencies, capital flows are a natural economic response to perceptions of higher financial returns. A real appreciation is called for in these cases. This is most easily and effectively achieved through a nominal appreciation. Efforts to block nominal appreciation in these cases would eventually result in a real appreciation through inflation, but this adjustment is likely to be delayed and costly. Countries can also use the classic remedy of fiscal tightening and monetary easing to reduce pressures on domestic interest rates and lower incentives for capital inflows, while maintaining domestic demand on a steady course.

The difficulty arises when capital is flowing to a country with an already overvalued exchange rate, with more than adequate levels of reserves, creating a risk that excess growth in credit or asset prices could leave the domestic financial system vulnerable. The challenge here is to contain the short-term risks without undermining the real long-term benefits that capital flows offer, and without distorting the market signals (and needed adjustments) that capital flows reflect.

But even in such extreme instances, measures to deter capital inflows should be seen only as a temporary fix and should be carefully structured to minimize distortionary or discriminatory effects. Experience has taught us that such measures are unlikely to have much lasting effect on aggregate flows, particularly as market participants find ways to evade their impact. There are also significant administrative costs for governments and compliance costs for firms.

At a systemic level, the imposition of capital controls and heavy foreign-exchange intervention in certain emerging-market economies has diverted capital flows to other economies that do not impose such measures, complicating policy management in these countries.

High-growth countries that have moved to more flexible exchange-rate regimes and more open capital accounts seem particularly vulnerable to such spillovers. We need to guard against negative externalities imposed by the proliferation of defensive measures against the free flow of capital. This is why a joint effort to develop a sensible consensus on approaches to be used in responding to surges is important.

Finally, the IMF has a crucial role to play in advancing this reform agenda. Through its surveillance role, the Fund can and should do more to promote more flexible exchange rates, a better balanced global economy, and more coherent management of volatile capital flows.

The IMF has long been an acknowledged center of expertise on international monetary issues. Accordingly, the G20 is relying on the Fund to play a key technical part in the G20 Framework for Strong, Sustainable, and Balanced Growth. Moreover, the Fund is working hard to strengthen its analysis on reserve adequacy and exchange-rate valuations,[4] which provide essential underpinnings for rigorous policy assessments. And the Fund is contributing to the task of developing sensible guidelines for managing capital flows based on a careful analytical framework and drawing lessons from cross-country experience.[5]

But the Fund must do more than provide high-quality technical analysis. It must also provide a stronger voice for globally coherent policies. The United States has long called for the IMF to strengthen its surveillance of exchange rates, and it remains critical for the Fund to follow through and speak more forcefully on exchange-rate issues. For a start, the IMF could increase transparency of surveillance by more widely publishing bilateral and multilateral surveillance products, such as by making publication of Article IV reports mandatory and publishing its exchange-rate assessments. But more than this, the Fund needs to make sure that its voice is forceful and candid. The recent report by the Independent Evaluation Office (IEO) of the IMF's performance in the run-up to the financial crisis makes clear that there is room for the Fund to do a better job at identifying and communicating risks to the global economy. This is about both sharpening the tools in the toolkit and also applying them more effectively to gain greater influence over policy decisions. This may require broader reforms of the Fund's governance structure to, in the words of the IEO report, "clarify . . . roles and responsibilities" and "establish a clear accountability framework."[6]

I end here by reiterating my central point: reform of the international monetary system is a key issue for today's global economic policy agenda, but to be most useful it should be directed squarely at delivering practical results to underpin a sustained and well-balanced global expansion.

Notes

1. G20 Leaders' Statement, The Pittsburgh Summit, September 24–25, 2009, http://www.g20.org/Documents/pittsburgh_summit_leaders_statement_250909 .pdf.

2. G20 Communiqué, Meeting of Finance Ministers and Central Bank Governors, Paris, February 18–19, 2011, http://www.g20.org/Documents2011/02/ COMMUNIQUE-G20_MGM%20_18-19_February_2011.pdf.

3. G20 Communiqué, Meeting of Finance Ministers and Central Bank Governors, Washington, DC, April 14–15, 2011, http://www.g20.org/Documents 2011/04/G20%20Washington%2014-15%20April%202011%20-%20final% 20communique.pdf.

4. See International Monetary Fund, "Addressing Reserve Adequacy," February 14, 2011, http://www.imf.org/external/np/pp/eng/2011/021411b.pdf.

5. See International Monetary Fund Staff Discussion Note, "Managing Capital Inflows: What Tools to Use," Jonathan D. Ostry et al., April 5, 2011, http://www .imf.org/external/pubs/ft/sdn/2011/sdn1106.pdf.

6. Independent Evaluation Office of the International Monetary Fund, Evaluation Report, "IMF Performance in the Run-Up to the Financial and Economic Crisis IMF Surveillance in 2004–07," 2011, http://www.ieo-imf.org/ieo/files/com- pletedevaluations/Crisis-%20Main%20Report%20(without%20Moises%20 Signature).pdf.

23

Liquidity and the International Monetary System

Maurice Obstfeld

In this chapter, I touch on points that are inspired by the crisis of 2008 to 2009, which displayed a number of stresses in the international system. Not surprisingly, these stresses are related to the problems that motivated the founding of the International Monetary Fund nearly seven decades ago.

Global liquidity needs, exchange rates, and external imbalances were fundamental problems in the interwar period and before, and the original design of the IMF devised ways to address these coordination problems within a framework that was appropriate to the economic and financial conditions of the time. But conditions have changed dramatically since the Bretton Woods era that ended in 1973. In fact, even over the course of the Bretton Woods era, the international economy evolved dramatically in ways that called into question the relevance of the settlement achieved at Bretton Woods in the 1940s. Here I focus on only one of many important issues—the liquidity issue.

One of the biggest changes to have occurred since World War II is financial globalization, the extent of which is unparalleled in history and far beyond what we had in the 1970s when the Bretton Woods system broke down. There are benefits to financial globalization but also immense risks, as we have seen recently. One of the key indicators of these risks is the very high level of gross external asset and liability positions in the world economy. These have grown explosively in the last couple of decades, and they bring currency mismatches and financial counterparty risks. If these risks are socialized, as they have been broadly across the world, they can become sovereign debt risks. Think of the case of Ireland. The globalization of capital markets has facilitated larger current-account imbalances, and those can also carry risks. The cases of

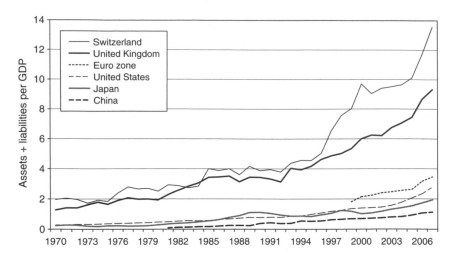

Figure 23.1
Gross external positions as a multiple of gross domestic product, 1970 to 2007.

Greece and arguably of the United States, too, illustrate some of those risks.

Consider the graphs of these gross positions in figure 23.1, showing external assets plus liabilities as a percentage of gross domestic product, from the updated Lane and Milesi-Ferretti (2007) data. The numbers for Switzerland, for example, approach fourteen times Swiss GDP toward the end of the data sample in 2007. We know the problems that the Swiss banks experienced. The major financial centers are bigger than other countries in this regard; smaller countries, like Ireland, can also have big ratios. Given these huge numbers, the implications of even smallish percentage losses, when the tab is picked up by governments, are frightening from a fiscal standpoint. Ireland well illustrates this problem.

In this context, the official institutional framework for providing international lending support has come to the fore. To safeguard financial stability, the crisis showed that we might need lender-of-last-resort support in multiple currencies, primarily the dollar but also other widely used international currencies.

An example of this need originated in the behavior of many European banks in the run-up to the crisis. They piled into the market for dollar-denominated asset-backed securities issued in the United States, funding their acquisitions with short-term wholesale dollar borrowing. You might have thought that their foreign-currency positions were hedged and that there was no mismatch, so no problem. But in fact, the liquidity and maturity transformation involved in these positions turned out to be very worrisome in the crisis, given the credit-market stresses that developed. Many banks in Europe found themselves unable to refinance their short-term dollar liabilities when credit markets and foreign-currency swap markets broke down. To make short-term dollar finance available to these banks, the Federal Reserve stepped in with dollar swap lines to foreign central banks. Other central banks established swap lines in their currencies.

Although the history of central-bank cooperation goes back at least to the early nineteenth century, these swap facilities were very different from most that we have seen before. In the 1960s, for example, the U.S. Treasury pioneered swap lines meant for balance-of-payments support, a fairly elaborate and, for a time, effective setup, but in the crisis we saw swap lines meant to channel true lender-of-last-resort assistance directly to beleaguered financial institutions.

The Federal Reserve became the dollar lender of last resort to the world, but this ad hoc role is unlikely to be preserved indefinitely because there are huge political obstacles to such an outcome. At one time, the perceived creditworthiness of the advanced markets made the lender-of-last-resort problem seem to be one of simply expanding conventional IMF lending and almost exclusively a problem of emerging-market and developing economies. But the crisis showed us that this is not so; the problem today is much broader than this.

For various reasons, depending on their individual experiences, emerging markets accumulated large reserves during the 2000s and found self-insurance to be one way of dealing with the risk of liquidity problems (figure 23.2). Emerging-market and developing-country reserves grew rapidly and have overtaken industrial-country reserves by quite a big margin, as this figure illustrates. Some reserves were used in the crisis, but the trend of rapid accumulation has hardly been affected. Some of this accumulation represents the side effects of intervention, and some of it is purposefully precautionary. It is hard to divide observed accumulation between the two motives.

This mechanism of self-insurance was advantageous at the individual-country level during the crisis, motivating policymakers in developing

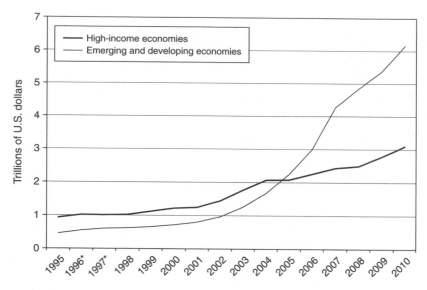

Figure 23.2
Global reserve holdings. *Source:* COFER database, International Monetary Fund (various years). *Note:* Years marked with * indicate a change in country average.

countries to continue to accumulate. But what is good for the individual is not necessarily good for the community, and there are many systemic drawbacks to self-insurance. There are also individual-country drawbacks, but the systemic drawbacks—drawbacks for the global financial system as a whole—are worrisome.

What are these systemic drawbacks? When you use reserves, you reallocate liquidity from other locations, so there is no creation of true outside liquidity in the system, as might be necessary in a crisis. Reserve accumulation can have asset-price effects—for example, when countries shift their reserve-currency choices on a large scale. And some reserves do not materially enhance financial stability. If you intervene to hold the exchange rate steady in the face of a short-term capital inflow, you increase short-term liabilities by the same amount as reserves. When the liabilities go, the reserves go. There is no increase in stability in that setting, but the volume of reserves is higher, and some of the perils of instability in world asset prices might be higher as well.

There are also neighborhood effects at work in determining reserve demand. If your neighbor holds more reserves than you, you may be viewed by markets as a more tempting target—the better place to sell assets in a crisis. For that reason, there will be an arms race—a tendency for countries to overaccumulate reserves. Finally, reserve accumulation may be deflationary if it is effected through higher current-account surpluses or policies that give rise to those.

Another systemic threat has been less recognized, and this is a modern-day version of the Triffin paradox. In the 1960s, the United States supported a growing stock of world dollar reserves on a narrow base of gold holdings. Although the United States promised to redeem those official reserves for gold at a fixed gold price, the system was unsustainable because to fulfill the underlying promise became impossibly expensive. A clear statement of Robert Triffin's updated paradox appears in a 2011 paper by Emmanuel Fahi, Pierre-Olivier Gourinchas, and Hélène Rey.

The reason for associating this new paradox with Triffin's name is that it likewise results from a similar inexorable dynamic. As a direct result of satisfying growing world demand for a reserve asset, an asset that is supposedly safe, the issuer eventually becomes unable to guarantee the reserve asset's safety. If reserve demanders prefer safe government debt, for example, then governments have to issue more debt. The assets the governments might hold as a counterpart will inherently be more risky. These might, for example, be claims on the private sector or foreign-currency claims. So there are fiscal limits on the ability of governments to satisfy the demand for safe reserves, just as there were limits in the 1960s on the ability of the United States to satisfy the world's demand for reserves while guaranteeing the reserves' value in terms of gold. The internal contradiction originates in some global economic asymmetries. First of all, considering economic growth rates, if we view the developing and emerging countries as the major demanders of reserves, they are simply growing much faster than the supposedly more creditworthy advanced economies. (The stronger credit of the advanced countries, making their governments' debts more eligible as reserve assets, is a second global asymmetry.) Lower-income countries now account for more than 50 percent of the world economy at purchasing power parity (PPP), and they are forecasted by the IMF and others to grow even bigger. If these countries keep accumulating reserves at the rate they have been, and if present growth trends continue as we expect, how will this demand for reserves possibly be satisfied?

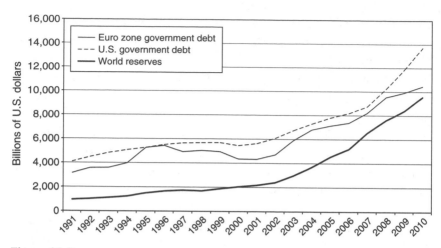

Figure 23.3
Global nongold reserves compared with gross general government debt. *Sources:* International Financial Statistics database (various years); World Economic Outlook database (various years).

One can get a rough idea of where the modern Triffin paradox stands today by looking at data like those in figure 23.3, which tracks reserves compared with the general government debts of the euro zone and the United States. This comparison is very crude, however, for a number of reasons. These are general and not central government debts, and certainly some euro zone central government debts (including those of Italy, Spain, Portugal, Ireland, and Greece) would hardly be viewed as safe reserve assets in the near term. Furthermore, countries may hold reserves in commercial banks. Those banks may be viewed as safe if there is an implicit bailout guarantee, but otherwise, they might be viewed as less than completely safe. (Again, the government's fiscal capacity is central to that assessment.) Syria and Brazil might have different views about where it is safe to hold their reserves. There are many interesting nuances here, but the basic point remains that the question of future reserve adequacy is a question of current relevance.

The international response to the recent crisis involved an expansion of IMF resources and potentially swifter responses through the flexible and precautionary credit lines. Those are useful innovations that need to be expanded and made more attractive relative to holding reserves, which provide unconditional and immediate liquidity. A major problem, unsurprising in view of past experience, is that very few countries have chosen to pre-qualify for these new IMF facilities.

The central-bank swap lines that sprang up during the crisis could and should be codified, as I and others have suggested (for example, Obstfeld 2009); there will certainly be need for them in the future. They could be run through the IMF directly to central banks that meet accepted standards of independence and supervisory efficacy. Or they could be run through the Bank for International Settlements (BIS). The conditionality and prequalification questions are critical for avoiding moral hazard.

Lending to central banks is different from sovereign lending, which has been the IMF's main role so far in its history. There is room for both types of crisis lending. If direct central bank loans were routed through the IMF rather than the BIS, the IMF's articles would need amendment. But there is precedent. When special drawing rights (SDRs) were introduced, they were quite a departure from what the IMF had generally done before.

SDRs amount to a reserve pooling arrangement. An SDR is essentially a claim on other IMF members' holdings of reserve currencies. It is hard for me to see why more explicit and expanded reserve pooling is not a more attractive option. In other words, why do we need the SDR to accomplish more effective reserve pooling? The SDR has evolved by default into a unit valued by a basket of currencies. That is not how it was originally defined, but when the par-value system disappeared in the early 1970s, there was a need to do something about the SDR's valuation, and the basket definition emerged as a convenient way to stabilize the unit's value against a particular reserve portfolio. The defining SDR basket started with sixteen currencies, then went to five, and then to four, which is where it stands now.

An advantage of having some sort of credit-line arrangements (on the model of the central-bank swap lines) is that they would diminish the dollar's singular role as a reserve currency. If you have credit lines in multiple currencies, you have access to all of those currencies and need not favor holdings of one over another. The dollar still has a dominant role as a vehicle currency in the private markets. It would be harder to dislodge from its vehicle currency role. I share others' reservations about the role of the SDR as a potential currency. It is not a currency currently, and to make it a currency would be difficult and would not be a natural development.

Discussion of the IMF's different roles and of the possibility of its acting on a larger scale raises the distinction between liquidity and solvency. The threat of institutional or sovereign insolvency has been an increasingly important factor in financial markets in recent years, and we still need to make progress in resolving sovereign debt and other crises as they come along. Having predictable resolution mechanisms in place is vital for containing moral hazard. Threats to close down big banks or to allow governments to restructure debts, however, cannot be credible without enhanced global supervision of the possibly systemically sensitive entities that lend to them. The crisis in the euro zone illustrates this.

I conclude with what I view as a deep moral of these discussions.

Much of what we mean when we talk about international monetary reform is institution building at a global level. This often seems impossibly hard, although we have made remarkable advances in that realm in the past. An institution like the International Monetary Fund would have been unthinkable without the experiences of the Depression and World War II. We should not need to experience calamities like those again to adapt our earlier achievements to the new and hazardous world that financial globalization has created.

A final question is manifest in the euro zone but also at the global level: whether national sovereignty and self-interest as expressed through democratic processes are inherently friendly to globalization. I believe that they are *not* inherently friendly to globalization, which is why we have supranational coordinating organizations such as the European Commission, the World Trade Organization, and the IMF. I therefore also believe that if we wish to support expanded globalization in our goods markets and our asset markets and perhaps eventually in labor markets, the globalization of governance institutions must expand as well, not only in liquidity provision but in other areas such as financial supervision.

This is the moral: economic globalization is limited by the globalization of governance.

References

Fahi, Emmanuel, Pierre-Olivier Gourinchas, and Hélène Rey. 2011. "Reforming the International Monetary System." Typescript (March). http://socrates.berkeley .edu/~pog/academic/FGR_march2011.pdf.

Lane, Philip R. and Gian Maria Milesi-Ferretti. 2007. "The External Wealth of Nations Mark II: Revised and Extended Estimates of Foreign Assets and Liabilities, 1970–2004." *Journal of International Economics* 73 (November): 223–250.

Obstfeld, Maurice. "Lenders of Last Resort in a Globalized World." 2009. *Monetary and Economic Studies* (Bank of Japan) 27 (November):35–52. http://www .imes.boj.or.jp/english/publication/mes/fmes.html.

Concluding Remarks

Olivier Blanchard

I took a lot of notes during the conference at which all these papers were presented and discussed. I organized my thoughts around the following nine points:

1. We have entered a brave new world. The economic crisis has put into question many of our beliefs. We have to accept the intellectual challenge.

2. In the age-old discussion of the relative roles of markets and of the state, the pendulum has swung, at least a bit, toward the state. We probably have revised our views on the need for regulation and on the limits of regulation. Both are stronger than we thought earlier.

3. The crisis has made it clear that many distortions are relevant for macro, many more than we thought earlier. We had ignored them, thinking that they were the province of microeconomists. But as we start to integrate finance into macro, we are discovering them anew. Agency theory is needed to explain how financial institutions work or do not work and how decisions are taken. Regulation and agency theory applied to regulators is also important. Behavioral economics and its cousin, behavioral finance, are central as well. With capital controls, for example, central issues are why investors are coming in or going out, what is behind their decisions, and how much herding plays a role in their decisions.

4. A theme that emerged from this conference is that macropolicy is a game (in the sense of game theory—policy is serious business) with many targets and many instruments. For example, a recurring theme in monetary policy has been that inflation stability alone is not enough; output stability and financial stability need to be added to the list. With fiscal

policy, we have to go from thinking about fiscal policy as just "government spending minus taxes" and an associated multiplier to realizing that there are 100 tools that can be used, that they have their own dynamic effects, and those effects depend on the state of the economy and other policies. I wonder whether we should not move the discussion away from multipliers. Working with multipliers makes you look for one number—if you only knew it, then you would be done—whereas we have to think of complex dynamic responses. Reducing discussions about fiscal policy to what is the right multiplier is not doing service to the issue (a point that Robert Solow makes in chapter 8).

The third example—again, I could choose many—is capital-account management. I like the provocative argument (made by Rakesh Mohan in chapter 15) that it may be possible to achieve the impossible trinity of an open capital account, a fixed exchange rate, and an independent monetary policy by using more instruments. Whether or not it can actually be done, using more instruments allows you to resolve, at least in principle, something that looks impossible with fewer instruments.

5. We may have many instruments, but we are not sure how to use them. In many cases, we are really uncertain about what they are, how they should be used, and whether they will work. Many examples came up during the various sessions at the conference. Liquidity ratios: because we do not know how to define liquidity in the first place, a liquidity ratio is one more step into the unknown. Capital controls: some people believe that they work and some people believe that they do not, and where you end up depends very much on that belief. Another example is Paul Romer's corollary to what he calls Myron's law, which is that if you adopt a set of financial regulations and keep them unchanged, the markets will find a way around them, and ten years later, you will have a financial crisis (chapter 12). Yet another example is Michael Spence's observations about the relative roles of self-regulation and regulation (chapter 19). Both are needed, and how we should combine them is extremely unclear.

6. Although these instruments are potentially useful, their use raises a number of political economy issues.

Some are hard to use politically. For cross-border flows, putting in place a regulatory structure is going to be difficult. Even at the domestic level, some of the macroprudential tools work by targeting a specific sector or a specific set of individuals or firms. This may lead to strong political backlash by the groups that are being directly targeted.

And instruments can be misused. The more instruments there are, the more the scope for misuse. Many people think that although there may be an economic case for capital controls, governments are going to use them instead of what they should be doing, which is choosing the right macroeconomic policy. Dani Rodrik argues for industrial policy as the right tool to increase the production of tradables without getting a current-account surplus (chapter 17). But in practice, the limits of industrial policy have not gone away.

7. Where do we go from here? In terms of research, the future is exciting. Many topics need work—namely, macro issues with (as Joseph Stiglitz, chapter 4, might say) the right microfoundations. For example, on capital controls, thinking of the exact source of distortions (if any) would allow for a much more informed discussion of the issues, a point that Ricardo Caballero makes forcefully in chapter 13.

8. Things are harder, I find, on the policy front. Given that we do not quite know how to use the new tools and they can be misused, how do policymakers go at it? Although we have to have a good sense of where we want to go in the end, a step-by-step approach is probably the way to do it. For example, I was critical of inflation targeting, but I do not think that one should, from one day to the next, give it up and move to a system with, say, five targets and seven instruments. We do not know how to do it, and it would be dangerous. Instead, we should introduce these macroprudential tools one by one or at least at a slow speed, see how they work, and then try to use them in the right way. But that process will take time.

Step by step is also the way to proceed in reforming the international monetary system. With SDRs, for example, it seems relatively easy to create a private market in private SDR bonds, see how it functions, and note whether it becomes deep enough to allow for large changes in supply and demand. If it is deep enough, one can think about a next step, such as having the IMF borrow by issuing SDR bonds to the private sector. If this turns out to be feasible, then one can think about the IMF doing this in times of systemic crisis to mobilize the funds needed to respond to large liquidity needs. All these steps have to be taken carefully.

A related point is that, in this new world, pragmatism is of the essence. That comes up, for example, in Andrew Sheng's discussion of the adaptive Chinese growth model (chapter 18). We have to try things carefully and see how they work.

9. We have to keep our hopes in check. There are going to be new crises that we have not anticipated and are not ready for. Despite our best efforts, we could well have old-type crises again. That is an interesting theme in Adair Turner's discussion of credit cycles (chapter 11). If we draw the implications from agency theory and put in place the right regulations, can we eliminate credit cycles? Or are they part of basic human nature, so that no matter what we do, they will come back in some form? I tend to be more of the second school than the first. So we need to be modest in our hopes.

A journalist asked me whether the conference on Macro and Growth Policies in the Wake of the Crisis was Washington Consensus 2. It was not intended to be, and it was not. It was the beginning of a conversation and an exploration. Time will tell where it takes us.

Contributors

Olivier Blanchard is the economic counselor and director of the Research Department at the International Monetary Fund.

Ricardo Caballero is the head of the Department of Economics, the Ford International Professor of Economics, and codirector of the World Economic Laboratory at the Massachusetts Institute of Technology and a National Bureau of Economic Research research associate in economic fluctuations and growth.

Charles Collyns serves as the U.S. Department of the Treasury's assistant secretary for international finance. In this position, Collyns is responsible for leading Treasury's work on international monetary policy, international financial institutions, coordination with the Groups of Seven, Eight, and Twenty, and regional and bilateral economic issues.

Arminio Fraga is chair and chief investment officer at Gavea Investimentos, an investment management firm based in Rio de Janeiro that he founded in August 2003.

Már Guðmundsson was appointed governor of the Central Bank of Iceland in 2009. Before taking that position, he was deputy head of the Monetary and Economic Department at the Bank for International Settlements and a member of the Bank's senior management.

Sri Mulyani Indrawati is managing director of the World Bank. She was formerly Minister of Finance of Indonesia (2005–2010).

Otmar Issing is president of the Center for Financial Studies (2006) and chair of the Advisory Board of the House of Finance at Goethe University, Frankfurt (2007).

Olivier Jeanne joined the Johns Hopkins Department of Economics in September 2008, after spending ten years in various positions in the Research Department of the International Monetary Fund.

Rakesh Mohan is professor of the practice of international economics and finance at the School of Management and senior fellow of the Jackson Institute for Global Affairs at Yale University, after serving as Deputy Governor of the Reserve Bank of India for several years.

Maurice Obstfeld is the Class of 1958 Professor of Economics at the University of California, Berkeley, and director of the Center for International and Development Economic Research.

José Antonio Ocampo is Professor at SIPA and Fellow of the Committee on Global Thought at Columbia University and formerly Minister of Finance of Colombia and former Under-Secretary-General of the United Nations for Economic and Social Affairs.

Guillermo Ortiz is Chairman of Grupo Financiero Banorte-IXE. He was governor of the Bank of Mexico (1998–2009, serving two consecutive six-year terms). In addition, he was Chairman of the Board of the Bank of International Settlements and previously served as Secretary of Finance and Public Credit in the Mexican Federal Government.

Y. V. Reddy was governor of the Reserve Bank of India from 2003 to 2008. Subsequently, he was a member of the United Nations Commission of Experts to the President of the U.N. General Assembly on Reforms of International Monetary and Financial System.

Dani Rodrik is the Rafiq Hariri Professor of International Political Economy at the John F. Kennedy School of Government, Harvard University.

David Romer is the Herman Royer Professor of Political Economy at the University of California, Berkeley. From February 2009 to September 2010, he was Senior Resident Scholar at the International Monetary Fund.

Paul M. Romer is the president of Charter Cities, a research nonprofit focused on the interplay of rules, urbanization, and development and Professor in the Stern School of Business, New York University.

Andrew Sheng has published widely in economics and finance. His latest publications are From Asian to Global Financial Crisis (Cambridge University Press, 2009) and an article on global financial regulatory reform in Global Policy 1(2) (May 7, 2010).

Hyun Song Shin is the Hughes-Rogers Professor of Economics at Princeton University.

Parthasarathi Shome is currently director and chief executive at the Indian Council for Research on International Economic Relations, New Delhi, after serving as Chief Economist at Her Majesty's Revenue and Customs, United Kingdom (2008–2011), and as Advisor to the Indian Finance Minister (2004–2008).

Robert Solow is professor emeritus at the Massachusetts Institute of Technology.

Michael Spence served as the chair of the Commission on Growth and Development (2006–2010), professor emeritus of management in the Graduate School of Business at Stanford University, a senior fellow of the Hoover Institution at Stanford, and professor of economics at the Stern School of Business at New York University. In 2001, he received the Nobel Prize in economic sciences.

Joseph Stiglitz is University Professor at Columbia University and the winner of the 2001 Nobel Prize for Economics. He served on President Clinton's economic team as a member and then chairman of the U.S. Council of Economic Advisors in the mid-1990s, and then joined the World Bank as chief economist and senior vice president.

Adair Turner was appointed chair of the Financial Services Authority (FSA) in September 2008 and chair of the Standing Committee on Regulatory Cooperation of the Financial Stability Board. He has combined careers in business, public policy, and academia.

Index

Note: An *f* or *t* following a page number indicates a figure or table.